NATURE TRAILS

by

Bob Cowgill

With Illustrations by Janet Ellis

(Events on Kiawah, A Barrier Island
on the Carolina Coast)

RIVERCROSS PUBLISHING, INC.
New York • Orlando

Printed in the United States of America. No part of this book may be used or reproduced in any manner whatsoever without written permission, except in the case of brief quotations embodied in critical articles and reviews. For information address RIVERCROSS PUBLISHING, INC., 127 East 59th Street, New York, NY 10022

ISBN: 0-944957-83-8

Library of Congress Catalog Card Number: 95-25998

Library of Congress Cataloging-in-Publication Data

```
Cowgill, Robert W. (Robert Warren), 1920-
    Nature trails : events on Kiawah, a barrier island on the Carolina
Coast / by Bob Cowgill ; with illustrations by Janet Ellis.
        p.   cm.
    Includes index.
    ISBN 0-944957-83-8 (pbk.)
    1. Natural history—South Carolina—Kiawah Island.    2. Seasons—
-South Carolina—Kiawah Island. 3. Kiawah Island    (S.C.)  I. Title.
Q.H.105.S6C68    1996                                          95-25998
508.757'91—dc20                                                    CIP
```

"As Thoreau found a universe in the woods around Concord, any person whose senses are alive can make a world of any natural place, however limited it might seem, on this subtle planet of ours."

Edward Abbey in Down the River.

Acknowledgments.

Many of these stories could not have been written without the numerous volunteers from among the island residents who made possible the protective program for turtle nesting on the beach. Only a few of these wonderful, concerned individuals could be mentioned by name in these stories; however, all of them know of my deep gratitude.

Thanks are due to those dedicated volunteers on the Bluebird nestbox brigade who provide for the birds that enliven our summers with their flashes of vivid blue.

Other stories could not have been written had it not been for the dedicated members of the South Carolina Department of Natural Resources (formerly the Wildlife and Marine Resources Department). The efforts of Sally and Tom Murphy, Charlotte Hope, Mark Dodd, John Cely, and Walt Rhodes have been especially protective of the wildlife on Kiawah, and I thank them all for allowing me to participate.

Among employees on the island, Major Baynard Seabrook of Security, Dylan Jones of the Recreation Department and Norm Shea as lagoon and pond manager have been mentioned in a number of these stories. They are continually involved in the protection of wildlife on the island and the skillful mediation between the wildlife and the increasing pressure of humans.

Finally, recognition should be given to that mythological cougar that haunts our sense of the mystery and wildness that still lingers on Kiawah.

Preface

The stories in this collection first appeared in Kiawah Island Talk, a monthly newspaper published by Kiawah Property Owners Group, Inc. for distribution to its members. They were written for a regular column, entitled Nature Trails, to inform members about events on Kiawah Island that relate to its natural beauty and the wildlife that share the island with us.

Kiawah Island, just south of Charleston, South Carolina, is one of the barrier islands that form a bulwark against the sea along the southern portion of the state. Ten miles of gently sloping beach face the Atlantic ocean, and a vast saltmarsh segmented by the Kiawah river separates the island from the mainland. Exciting events occur on the beach and in the marsh at all seasons of the year. Also, there are the lively doings, sometimes amusing and sometimes tragic, of the numerous animals and birds that visit and in many cases live year-round in the lagoons and forests of live oak, pine and palmetto. All have constituted grist for the mill that is Nature Trails.

It is my hope that the collection will renew cherished memories for faithful readers of the column, and bring to new readers an awareness of the drama of living on a tiny barrier island.

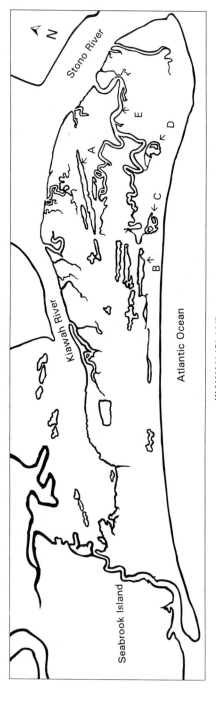

KIAWAH ISLAND

A: Blue Heron Pond   B: Canvasback Pond
C: Ibis Pond   D: Willet Pond
E: Bass Creek

Table Of Contents

Fall of 1992 9
Rattlesnake - Turtles - Migratory Ducks

Winter of 1992 19
Food Sources - Alligators - Turtle Nesting - White Ibis

Spring of 1993......................................29
Owls - Cabin - Red Knots - Beach Stabilization

Summer of 1993 35
Dolphins - Turtle Nesting Goes Volunteer - Laughing
Gulls

Fall of 1993 45
Buck Deer - Dune Plants - Cougar - Turtle Nesting -
Great Blue Heron - Bufflehead Pond

Winter of 1993 55
Feeding Habits of Birds - Pelicans in Winter - Whale

Spring of 1994......................................63
Marsh - Owls - Turtle Nesting - Portuguese
Man-of-War

Summer of 1994 71
Least Terns - Turtle Nesting - Ospreys - Leatherback

Fall of 1994 81
Whale - Not-So-Wildlife - Pelicans - Dune Plants - A
Duck Out of Water

Winter of 1994 89
Wood Storks - Island History - Distemper - Turtles -
Ducks

Spring of 1995......................................99
Marsh - Owls - Turtle Mating - Swallow - Whales

Summer of 1995 109
Turtle Hatching - Cardinal Behavior - Combat! -
Distressed Hawk Chick - Alligator Nest

Fall of 1995..119
Beach History - Frogs - Least Terns - Ridley Turtle

Winter of 1995 127

Tidalmarsh - Ospreys - Sea-rocket - Mixed Flocks

Index 135

FALL, 1992

Yes, There Are Snakes in Paradise.

Mike Quinn was taking his two Labrador retrievers for a walk on the beach near the exit at Osprey Beach development about 4 PM on October 15th. Suddenly they encountered a coiled rattlesnake about 20 feet above the water line. Before Mike could prevent it, the black lab named Woody approached the snake and was struck twice in the face. Mike was greatly concerned about Woody, of course, and rushed off the beach at once. He and his wife drove off the island, stopping only momentarily at the main gate to get directions to the nearest veterinarian. Despite all efforts, Woody died of what the veterinarian termed a massive injection of venom. I'm sure all of us share the sadness of the Quinn family over the loss of Woody, who was a member of the family and Mike's hunting companion. As Mike said to me, "Kiawah was paradise for us; now it is paradise lost." Let's hope that with time paradise will be restored.

What of the snake? Mike, who has had some experience with reptiles in various lands, prudently had not approached it but estimated its weight at 20-25 lbs. and of a diameter of 3 or 3 ½ inches. From the size, the massive amount of venom, and the skin pattern, it was probably an Eastern Diamondback rattlesnake—one of the six most dangerous snakes in the world. The snake did not uncoil while Mike was there, but from written descriptions of the species it was probably 6 to 8 feet in length.

What caused this very unusual occurrence of a venomous snake on the beach? Construction was underway nearby on a new road just before Flyway Drive connects with Governor's Drive. The noise and powerful vibrations of the heavy machinery may have driven the snake from its normal habitat, and as it tried to flee it ended up on the beach. (I remarked to Nancy, my wife, that it was stressed out; she replied that it probably was hypervenomating.)

This leads to the next questions, what kinds and numbers of poisonous snakes are there on Kiawah Island, and what precautions should be taken? The Environmental Inventory of Kiawah Island published in 1975, listed 14 different species of snakes on the island. Because the general habitat remains the same, it is probable that a similar number remain today. The non-venomous snakes far out-number the venomous and should be protected for reasons we may explore at another time. The venomous ones that might be encountered on Kiawah are the Copperhead, Cottonmouth and three species of rattlesnake (Eastern Diamondback, Timber and Pigmy). Construction workers who cut the new roads and golf course maintenance staff inform me that most of these snakes flee if at all possible. The one exception is the Cottonmouth, which can be quite aggressive. Unfortunately, the Cottonmouth is the one snake most likely to be encountered by golfers searching for golf balls along lagoon banks, and they should always bear this hazard in mind. But in general, venomous snakes prefer habitats not usually trespassed by humans (although subject to trespass by dogs not on leash). Disturbance of their habitat by flooding or heavy construction could drive them into developed areas, as may have been the case mentioned at the beginning of this story. Also, snakes seek a warm surface, particularly on cold nights in the fall. It is then that one might choose a poorly lighted walkway or driveway that had been warmed by the sun during the day. We should take suitable precautions and also warn our visitors of the possibility of such an encounter.

One precaution that all can take is to be familiar with the appearance of the venomous species. An adequate and very inexpensive guide is one of the paperback Golden Nature Guide series, *Reptiles and Amphibians* that is available in most book stores. If you are ever in doubt, Major Seabrook of Security assures me that they welcome calls and will send someone out as soon as possible to examine and remove a snake on the property.

Loggerhead, the Marine Turtle that Nests on Kiawah Island

Five species of marine turtles, the Green, Hawksbill, Kemp's ridley, Leatherback and Loggerhead, pass by our shore, but only the Loggerhead nests here. You may never see it come ashore because that normally occurs at night, but the biologists can give a good description. The Loggerhead (*Caretta, caretta,* to give it the definitive scientific name) is quite variable in size, measuring from possibly 30 to 47 inches of carapace (top shell) length and weighing about 300 lbs. for the adult female and 400 lbs. or more for the male. It has a massive, blunt head from which it derives its name, for sailors upon seeing the raised head in the water often mistook it for a log. The outermost layer of plates on the shell and head are called scutes, and the number and position of the scutes are used to distinguish the various species. The Loggerhead is the most abundant of the five species in the western Atlantic, and it wanders widely in tropical and sub-tropical waters where it feeds on sponges and algae.

Loggerheads are of an ancient lineage, because their ancestors go back more than 150 million years. Today, their ancient lifestyle is threatened by human activities all over the world. The genetic traits and behavioral characteristics they developed over those vast periods of time made their survival possible. However, those traits are not flexible enough to permit them to adapt to the swift and drastic changes inflected upon their habitat by the recent arrival of man. Therefore, many of us feel impelled to do what we can to insure that they continue to survive and share with us this beautiful world they have known so very long.

The first protection of a Loggerhead turtle rookery that I am aware of was begun by property owners of Little Cumberland Island, Georgia in 1964. Shortly thereafter, other private groups began protecting their rookeries, and the Kiawah Island program in 1972 was one of the early ones. Since 1978, the Loggerhead has been listed as a threatened species under the Federal Endangered Species Act of 1973. Now, it is protected under both the Federal act and the South Carolina Nongame and Endangered Species Program during all stages of its life cycle. After the governmental actions were taken, the private groups have continued to protect the nesting in cooperation with the government agencies.

Enough about human activity, both good and bad; let's consider the nesting process from the point of view of the Loggerhead turtle. As the water warms on the continental shelf in spring, male and female turtles assemble and slowly move toward shore to mate. After mating, the male departs and where he goes no man knows. Suffice to say that the female remains offshore while her fertilized eggs develop. About May, after the water has warmed further, she lumbers ashore at night and begins the laborious struggle up the beach to a nesting site. She is wary at this time and easily frightened off by a noise or a carelessly shown flashlight; that is one reason we have the motto, "Lights out for turtles."

Once she has selected a site, she digs her nest with her back flippers, alternating one and then the other to withdraw a scoop of sand until she reaches the maximum depth, usually about 18 inches beneath the surface. Then she begins to deposit her eggs, one at a time, which fall to the bottom of the nest and pack together. Once the process has begun, she will continue even if disturbed by enthusiastic people shining lights in her eyes or equally enthusiastic raccoons stealing eggs at the rear. When the last of the 100-150 eggs have been deposited, she tops off the nest with sand, packs it down firmly by thumping her shell over it and throws sand all around the area with her flippers for concealment. Down the beach and into the waves she goes, never to return to the nest. She has done her part; now it is up to the next generation.

However, she doesn't do this just once in a season. After about 2 weeks another clutch of eggs will develop from the original mating, and once again, and probably for a third and fourth time, she will trudge ashore to make other nests. Where is she during those periods between nestings? Information is fragmentary but the few radio-tagged females seem to wander about in local waters, and scuba divers often find them asleep beneath ledges close inshore. Finally, her nesting duties complete, she departs for the ocean. Then, she may skip a year or two before repeating the performance.

What happens in the nest she has left behind? Assuming that she has chosen a safe site, the eggs begin to develop. Each egg is remarkably like a ping-pong ball in appearance. It is round, white and covered with a parchment-like, pliable shell. The dark, moist nest cavity beneath the sand maintains a constant temperature day and night; therefore, it is a nearly ideal incubation chamber. The temperature is maintained in part by the warmth of the sand and in part by the heat generated by the metabolic activity in the eggs. Temperature influences the length of incubation and is critical in determination of the sex of the hatchlings. At 29° C. (84° F) the hatchlings are male and female in equal numbers; a few degrees higher, and the proportion is mainly female; a few degrees lower, it is mainly male.

The embryo draws nourishment from the yolk and develops over a period of about 55 days into a tiny turtle, all curled up within the shell. It grows a sharp spine on the tip of its snout called an egg tooth, and with that tooth it ruptures the shell and is able to leave the egg. Resting, sometimes for days within the nest cavity, it straightens its body and continues to consume the remnant of the yolk sac which is still attached.

Then, restless stirring within the compact mass of little turtles activates them all, and they cooperatively struggle up through the sand to within perhaps a few inches of the surface. There they pause and wait again. What are they waiting for? They wait for the best time to leave the nest and make a dash for the ocean; that time is after nightfall when most predators are not around or least likely to see them. They seem to sense that time by the drop in temperature of the surface sand as the sun goes down. Then out they come in a rush and head for the water. How do they know which way to go? They head for the brightest mass they see for in ancient times the brightest mass on a beach was the wave-tops catching the light from the moon and stars. Today, unfortunately, they may head instead toward a home or street light with tragic results. Once again, a reason for the motto, "Lights out for turtles."

Their scurrying trip down the beach to the water seems to set their guidance system and is essential; if they are carried down by misguided folks who want to save them the trip, the poor things circle round and round in the water as though bewildered. Once they reach the water on their own, they instantly change from a crawling gait to a swimming stroke and off they go as rapidly as possible. Here too the predators await because they are a welcome morsel for fish and crabs beneath the surface and for gulls and other birds above.

For a long time it was a mystery where they went. Now we are beginning to understand that they swim away from land in a frenzy until they encounter masses of sargassum and other seaweeds possibly 20-30 kilometers offshore. Here in the shelter of the weed, they remain and grow for an indeterminate length of time; then, they voyage out on their own into the vast ocean, navigating possibly by magnetic signals and wave direction. After a period of 20-25 years the few survivors (perhaps one in ten thousand!) will gather off the coast to mate and nest. Hopefully they will receive a friendly and protective reception at that time from our children and grandchildren.

Migratory Ducks Will Soon Arrive for the Winter

It is important that those of us living on Kiawah Island should be aware of the waterfowl that visit our ponds and lagoons each winter after their long flights from the north. Aside from the pleasure of seeing these beautiful birds, both in flight and on the ponds, they tell us something important about the state of health of our environment. Unlike the caged canaries that were carried beneath ground to warn miners of carbon monoxide gas in the mine shafts, the waterfowl are free to travel where they wish. Their presence assures us that the pond environment is healthy. Interestingly enough, it is possible to turn this around and consider the maintenance of these southern ponds in good condition as a means of preserving our duck species. It is important to protect the summer nesting ponds in the north as has been well publicized, but in a way it is equally important to provide the migratory ducks a safe environment for their sojourn in the south in the winter. And this is just what Kiawah Island seems to be doing.

The island has over 100 ponds and lagoons that range from many small ones of a fraction of an acre in size to large ponds such as Bass (33 acres) and Willet (40 acres). The ponds vary in depth, vegetation, salinity and other characteristics that make them more or less attractive for migratory ducks. The newer and generally smaller lagoons were created during the development of golf courses and real-estate and many of them do not have the protective vegetation and food resources to attract ducks. The older ponds were created about thirty or forty years ago by diking off fingers of marsh that lay between the ancient dunes that formed the island. Mr. Thomas C. Welch, Jr., the island caretaker from 1958 to 1973, tells me that the ponds were stocked with fish but were not intended to draw waterfowl for hunting. Over the years, however, vegetation has grown in these older ponds and now serves as protective cover and food for the ducks. To the degree that these conditions can be maintained in the future, ducks should continue to visit us each winter.

I recently concluded a report on the migratory ducks that I observed over a period from 1981 to 1992. (for those of you who might wish to examine the report, *A Survey of Migratory Ducks on the Ponds of Kiawah Island, South Carolina from 1981 to 1992*, it is on file at the office of the town of Kiawah Island.) The clearest conclusion to come from the study is that the migratory ducks are giving Kiawah Island good marks for the quality of some of the ponds. Their presence on the ponds, both in diversity of species and in numbers, will bear this out. The range of 7-14 species present each year showed no significant increase or decrease in the last few years, and the total of 19 species that were seen on the island during the entire decade is all that might be expected on ponds in the Charleston area. The Wood duck was rarely seen even though it is fairly common in the state; however, it prefers freshwater ponds and perhaps the ponds on Kiawah are too saline. Scaup and Scoter are sea ducks that do not normally occur on inland ponds and were not included in the report. They come down from the north in huge flocks and spend the winter just offshore.

The total number of other migratory ducks varied widely from 183 in 1987 to 694 in 1983 and this reflects the annual variations seen for the state and the southeast in general. In part the variation also may be caused by unusually large flocks of one or another species on the island in some years. For example, the year 1987 of lowest total number was a year without a large number of any one species. By contrast, the year 1983 of a very high total population was also a year in which there were 274 American Wigeon on the island. Hooded Merganser and Green- winged Teal also visit us from time to time in large flocks. For example, a flock of over 200 Hooded Mergansers stayed on Blue Heron pond for seven weeks in the winter of 1991-1992. Possibly the food supply of small fish became exhausted and accounted for their departure. In support of this supposition, no waterfowl descended upon Blue Heron pond in March of 1992 when it was drawn down; normally these birds then feast on the small fish concentrated in the remaining pools of water. Therefore, it would appear that the fish had already been consumed by the Hooded Mergansers.

Alligators probably take some ducks but the birds do not seem to be frightened off a pond by the presence of alligators. In fact, ducks of several species have been observed resting and feeding within a few yards of alligators on the banks. When alligators or river otters are in the water, ducks keep a wary eye on them and move out of the way but seldom take flight. Bobcats, eagles and some of the larger hawks are other natural predators that the ducks have always had to avoid. The human predator, the poacher, was present on the island in the early 1980's but did not seem to reduce the population significantly nor drive the ducks away for any length of time.

It is encouraging that some species are becoming habituated to human disturbance. Three examples from 1992 observations will be given. In March, 32 Green-winged Teal were on Pintail pond along with numerous other waterfowl. Despite the noise of a tractor mower running along the golf fairway beside the pond, the ducks only moved farther away on the water except for five that flew to a quieter section of the same pond. Similarly, small flocks of Bufflehead have been observed on Ibis pond swimming past a lot with all the noise associated with house construction. And finally, a small flock of Hooded Mergansers has spent the winter on a 3-acre pond at Governor's Drive and Trumpet Creeper Lane that has seven homes, one road with light traffic and another road with heavy traffic on its perimeter. Therefore, some of the species may disappear due to reduction in population nation-wide or be too shy to tolerate the human activity on Kiawah, but others should continue to return and add beauty and vitality to our ponds.

WINTER, 1992

Winter Food Sources for Our Wildlife.

Twenty two members of the Naturalist's Club toured Mingo Point one sunny morning in October to determine what food sources might be available for birds and other animals in that natural setting. While doing so, they were rewarded by a perfect V of Canada geese flying overhead and a flock of Skimmers swiftly flying low over the river and flashing their characteristic black and white wing pattern. A total of twenty-five different species of trees, bushes, vines and herbs were found bearing nuts, seeds and other fruits that wildlife will depend upon for food this fall and winter. Most of these plants were found at the edge of wooded areas where conditions for growth are good. Similar edges for good growth of these same plants are to be found along most of the major roadways on the island.

Look but Do Not Touch!

A large number of Portuguese Man-of-War were seen on our beach just before Thanksgiving. Millions of these normally ride the Gulf Stream as it flows north along our coast. If there have been several days of prevailing winds during the winter, many can be driven in-shore. On the beach, the animal resembles a small, partially deflated blue balloon, but that float is resting on a mass of tentacles that may extend 40-50 feet and are loaded with stinging cells. Admire its beauty but do not touch.

Nuisance Alligators in 1992.

An alligator is termed a nuisance alligator by both our Security department and the state Wildlife & Marine Resources Department if it meets the following three criteria. #1: It is of a potentially dangerous size (greater than five feet). #2: It is without fear and possibly even aggressive (because of having been fed) or sick and lethargic (then it is easily approached and totally unpredictable in behavior). #3: It is in an area that is heavily populated, particularly by children and/or pets. Major Seabrook of our Security force, who has had special training in alligator control procedures, makes the ultimate decision on removal. Often he is kind enough to bring me along for a "second opinion" on the case.

In 1992, a total of eight large alligators had to be removed, and this compares with seven in 1991 and five in 1990. In addition, two others died in 1992; one was run over by an automobile and the second was found dead of unknown cause on the Ocean golf course. Four smaller ones, of four feet or less, were relocated to other ponds on Kiawah. Probably all of these returned to their original ponds in a few days, but the trauma of removal seems to have made them wary of humans and no longer a nuisance.

How can we decrease the number that must be removed and destroyed? Best is probably the education of all visitors to our island on the nature of these animals and the importance of not feeding or harassing them. Another approach is to give at least some of them a safe haven in refuges.

Bald Eagle Sighting for The January Survey

Last month you were asked to be on the look-out for eagles on the island in January for the annual survey by the wildlife department I am aware of only two sightings early in the month. One adult Bald eagle was seen on the 2nd and I noted an immature Bald eagle on the 3rd of the month. The immature one was at the very western end of the island, in fact, it was perched on a tree across the Kiawah river so really it's a "Seabrook" eagle.

History of the Early Years of the Protective Program for Loggerhead Turtle Nesting on Kiawah Island.

Introduction

Protection of nests of the Loggerhead turtle on Kiawah Island dates back to 1972 so the 1992 season was the 20th anniversary of continuous protection. There have been large changes in procedures during that time and one period when the program faltered and nearly expired; therefore, this is an opportune time for an extensive review.

The nesting site, called a rookery, probably dates back to the creation of the island thousands of years ago, and there is evidence that turtles were a part of the culture of coastal Indians as long ago as 4000 years. Certainly the Kiawah Indian tribe must have known of the nesting site. Its existence also must have been known to the European settlers in the 18th and 19th centuries, and they probably joined the other natural predators in raiding the nests. Persons still living in this area relate that it was customary for people from Johns Island and Charleston to visit the beach and probe with sharpened sticks for nests that the raccoons had missed. Indeed, it was not until the second half of this century that people began to abandon the practice and consider the necessity of protecting nests of this threatened species. Even as late as 1973 egg poaching by humans occurred once on Kiawah Island and was thwarted once. No known poaching has occurred on the island since that date.

1972-1975

Much of the story of these early years comes from personal recollections of persons involved in the events or living on the island and familiar with the endeavor. Protection and study of the turtle rookery originated through the actions of two young friends in Charleston who had long shared an interest in reptiles. O. Rhett Talbert, Jr. and Tom McGee were unaware that the Loggerhead was a threatened species when they became interested in the animal and decided in 1972 to spend their summer break from college observing its nesting behavior. They received permission and encouragement from Mrs. C.C. Royal who with her children owned the island at that time. The two then approached the South Carolina Wildlife & Marine Resources Dept., and received a modest sum for supplies and the use of an old Jeep for patrolling the beach at night. They counted emergent crawls, and attempted to make correlations between the number of crawls and phases of the moon, tidal stage, and time of night.

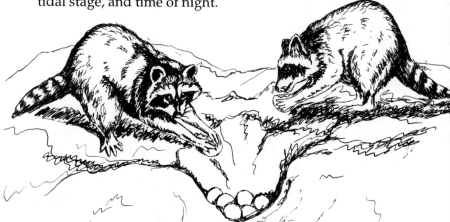

As the study progressed, they were dismayed by the nearly total destruction of nests by raccoons, and they began putting 3' × 3' screens of hardware cloth of 2" × 4" mesh size over the nests as protection. Even so, some predation of nests continued despite the screens. One night as they were patrolling the dark beach for tell-tale marks of new turtle crawls, they observed an adult raccoon eating an egg over a screened nest. Intrigued as to how it could reach the eggs, they approached and in the light from the headlights saw the adult leave and an immature kit come up from the nest, pass through the screen, and trot off after the adult. Presumably the kit was passing eggs up to its parent. On the basis of this observation, they began to protect the nests further with a smaller screen of finer mesh placed in the center of the large one.

From their efforts that summer, they obtained a research grant from the National Science Foundation to support their further studies. During the summer of 1973 they enlisted four more friends into the enterprise, and the study continued along the same lines as in 1972 but was enlarged to include the tagging of female turtles in an effort to determine the number of turtles using the rookery. To prevent the continuing loss of nests to raccoons, a hatchery was installed which consisted of a wire enclosure located in the secondary dune field.

In 1974 and 1975 an extensive environmental inventory of the island was sponsored by the Kuwait Investment Co. at the time of purchase of Kiawah Island for development. Among the many aspects of the natural environment that were evaluated was the turtle-nesting on the beach. John Dean of the Belle Barusch Institute and Rhett Talbert were the logical ones to do that evaluation. Supported by funds for the environmental inventory, Rhett continued his ongoing studies. In 1974 nests in the hatchery were destroyed by extremely heavy rains that flooded Kiawah Island with an estimated 20 inches of rain in the first twenty days of August. Only nine nests hatched. This destruction prompted a change in 1975 to a new "shed" hatchery. Eggs were packed in styrofoam coolers, stored in a shelter, and periodically moistened. Hatchlings were released above the high water mark at various locations on the beach in the evening within 24 hours of emergence from the sand, and it was concluded that this was the most satisfactory protective measure for the future.

1976-1979

Then followed a period from 1976 through 1979 for which most records have been lost. What is clear is that the program continued with a hatchery for protection of the nests. The program was supported by the Kiawah Island Co. through the Kiawah Island Community Assoc., and the change in support was marked by a shift in emphasis on objectives. Hatchery production and resort guest education became the primary objectives. The tagging program was abandoned and nesting data collection was erratic. It was during this period that the Federal Endangered Species Act included the Loggerhead as a threatened species and the S. C. Wildlife & Marine Resources Dept. became involved in protection of this and other threatened or endangered species along the S.C. coast. However, the state was not involved on Kiawah Island until about 1980 when it began issuing permits to operate the protective programs. It was then that annual reports appeared on a regular basis, because this was one of the requirements for the permit.

1980-1985

Beyond 1980, annual reports have been preserved, and the following accounts are from them. The beach was patrolled throughout the night, and as has been customary ever since that time, no other vehicles were allowed access at night. The 1982 season was a period of program reevaluation, and an emphasis was placed once again on data collection. Operations for the 1983 season reflected further changes with focus on three main objectives:

1) conservation of the species;

2) public education;

3) comprehensive data collection.

As an illustration of the scope of the operation at this time, the 1985 Community Association budget allotted $15,000 for the turtle program including salaries for four patrol and hatchery personnel.

A public education program was initiated and vigorously pursued. The two components of the program were evening slide shows and patrol tours. For example, in 1983 the slide shows were presented twice each week throughout the summer to discuss the natural history of the turtle and the nesting program on Kiawah. The tours with the night patrols were limited only by the number that could be crammed into the patrol jeep and seem to have to have been quite popular (more than 200 persons participated in 1983.)

1986-1987

We now come upon a dark period in the story. The curtain began to come down in 1986 when the Kiawah Island Co. was primarily interested in selling the island and neglected the program. William Botts, known to most people on the island as Buzz was the unsung hero at this time. Buzz directed the Jeep Safari operations and probably some of you encountered him as one of the most pleasant and knowledgeable of the guides. Buzz had participated in the turtle program for several years and in 1986 he operated it with one other paid employee.

In 1987 Buzz again contracted to operate the program, but it was abruptly cancelled a few days prior to the beginning of the nesting season. The reason was a budget "shortfall." Finally, in mid-June, operations began but with a very restricted scope because of the shortfall. The hatchery was eliminated, as well as the lectures; patrols were changed to once daily at dawn, and the personnel numbered two. Despite all these handicaps Buzz prevailed and a very creditable report was written for the last portion of the year.

The protective program did not quite founder at that stage despite the stormy seas, and later I will relate how it was rescued.

Beach Erosion.

A combination of high tides plus off-shore winds and waves have cut deeply into our beach and created nearly vertical banks that are in some places higher than six feet. Some may philosophically shrug and say, "The sea giveth and the sea taketh away." But the turtle folks offer prayers to the Mother of All Turtles,

> "May the banks melt away
> Before the turtles come in May."

White Ibises Are Among Our Winter Visitors.

The White ibis is a wading bird that you are most likely to encounter in winter along a lagoon edge, although it will occasionally be found on the golf fairways. It is about the size and color of the smaller of our white egrets, the Snowy, but may be readily distinguished by its down-curved orange beak. Both the white adult birds and the greyish-brown immatures may be seen, often in mixed flocks. These flocks usually number twenty or less; however, last winter I counted 98 in one immense flock at Blue Heron Pond and encountered a flock of 37 along the Ocean Course this winter. On the golf fairways, they search for insects, but in their normal habitat along the lagoon banks they forage for crayfish, crabs, molluscs and small snakes.

They are such energetic foragers that they stir up all sorts of prey in the vicinity. This gives rise to a commensal relationship with other birds and you will often see one or more of the egrets or herons following along closely behind the busy ibises. The egret or heron often will snatch prey frightened to the surface but beyond the ibis' reach. In turn, the taller and more alert egret often warns the shorter and less wary ibis of approaching predators. Similar commensal relationships are common even between vastly different species; one that most of us are familiar with is that of the Cattle egrets that attend grazing cattle and snatch the insects stirred into motion by the animal's hooves, another is the ant birds that fly above columns of army ants in the tropics.

In flight, the White ibis is a magnificent sight as it flies along with its head and neck extended. With the dramatic pattern of black wing tips on an otherwise white body, it resembles a scaled down version of the Wood stork that occasionally visits our island in lesser numbers. As the ibises leave us in spring, the flocks head for nesting rookeries where they may congregate in the tens of thousands. Several years ago there was a rookery on Drum Island in the Cooper river, but this is no longer a suitable site and all the herons and egrets as well as the ibises have abandoned it. Most likely the ibises that winter here now travel to the large rookery on Lake Marion.

Sea Ducks May Be Seen From the Beach.

In the last part of January immense flocks of sea ducks numbering in the thousands could be seen from the beach either floating in dark clusters called rafts on the surface of the water or flying in long black skeins silhouetted against the pearly white clouds of winter. The ones I saw are Scaup. How they acquired such an unattractive name is not known for certain. Possibly it is a rendition of the bird's call; if the poor bird had a more melodious voice it might have been called a bobolink. Sea ducks come down from the north in the winter and may stay off our beach for days or weeks at a time before shifting farther along the coast. They will not return north until spring. Other species that we might expect from time to time are Black scoters and Surf scoters. All feed upon tiny molluscs and crustaceans in the shallow water.

Great Horned Owls Are Our Earliest Nesters.

The only Osprey nest that I'm aware of that produced young on Kiawah last year has been taken over this winter by a pair of Great Horned owls for their winter nesting. (Why owls and the Bald eagle nest in winter rather than the mild spring season, I will try to answer in a later story.) It is not unusual for these owls to move into a nest constructed earlier by a crow or hawk family and make it their own. The usurpation of an osprey nest is rather a bold and perhaps even a foolhardy undertaking by the owls. It will be quite interesting to see how the Ospreys respond in the next month when they find that the nest they so laboriously constructed last year is now occupied. It is at the top of a dead pine snag about a quarter of a mile west of Willet Pond. The nest may be seen with the unaided eye but a spotting scope will be needed to really see the owl with its prominent "horned ears" and the two chicks that are now peering over the nest rim at their new world.

SPRING, 1993

Owl Nesting Update.

To my astonishment, the owl nest survived the fury of the Blizzard of '93. Shortly after the storm passed, the nest appeared empty, but that was just because the two owlets were huddled so far down. The next day they were both up and stomping about in the nest as though impatient for mommy to arrive with breakfast. The original owners of the nest, the ospreys, apparently decided to give up gracefully and are renovating an older nest about a quarter of a mile away across Bass creek.

Continuing Saga of the Great Horned Owls.

In April another chapter unfolded in the development of the Great Horned owl family that occupied the old osprey nest near Willet pond. On the day before Easter, both owlets were together in the nest, but on Easter morning the nest was empty. Often young owls of this species fall or leap out of the nest before they can fly, and the parents continue to feed and protect them as they huddle together on the ground or find shelter in low brush or a fallen tree. Thinking that such might have befallen the two in this case, I set out on Monday afternoon to search for them. It was a beautiful day for such an adventure, and the quarter mile hike through the woods did not seem formidable despite the brush and downed trees left over from hurricane Hugo. As I beat my way through the brush and over or under tree trunks, however, I suddenly became aware that the two parent owls were above me in the top of a tall pine tree. Viewed at that closeness, each seemed larger than any owl ought to be, and they looked for all the world like two large bobcats with their ears perked up. Silently they watched my labored progress, and as I approached the foot of the dead pine

that contained the nest, I remembered an account of the aggressiveness of this species when eggs or young are threatened.

"Swiftly the old bird came straight as an arrow from behind and drove her sharp claws into my side, causing a deep dull pain and unnerving me, and no sooner had she done this than the other attacked from the front and sank his talons deep into my right arm causing blood to flow freely, and a third attack and my shirt sleeve was torn to shreds for they had struck me a third terrible blow on the right arm tearing three long deep gashes, four inches long, also one claw went through the sinew of my arm, which about paralyzed the entire arm."

(From an account by Donald J. Nicholson as quoted in Life Histories of North American Birds of Prey, by Arthur C. Bent, Part II, page 314.)

Fortunately I did not receive such a ferocious reception, for the parents knew full well that their babies were not lying helpless at the foot of the nest tree. Scanning trees in the vicinity with binoculars, I finally located one of the owlets, much fluffier and smaller than the parents and with the ear tufts scarcely discernible. It was about 80 feet up in a pine tree probably 300 yards from the nest tree. I suspected that the other owlet would be nearby and spotted it shortly in a neighboring tree; it appeared to be appreciably larger than the first and distinctly cinnamon in general color. It was quite a thrill to stand in one spot and view the entire family of four at the same time.

While scanning the trees for the young owls, I had noticed the carcass of what appeared to be a Clapper rail lodged about 60-70 feet up in the crotch of still another pine tree. Whether it had been placed there by one of the parent owls as food for the young, I cannot say but it was a remarkable place to find a marsh rail!

Will we have another installment: That is, will the ospreys reclaim their old nest in its present deplorable state? Time will tell.

The Cabin by Willet Pond.

The old cabin by Willet pond has an interesting history that needs to be told before the cabin finally collapses from neglect and vandalism. Several years ago it was in much better shape, and has long served as a landmark so that when you sighted it you knew you were at Willet pond rather than the similar pond, Ibis, farther to the west. Once the vandals were able to tear off the locked door, the pace of destruction has accelerated.

Now for the history, which I have learned from Thomas Welch, Jr. of Charleston. He was caretaker of the island from 1958 until the Royal family sold it to the Kuwait Investment Company in 1974. Even prior to that period of time, Tom and his dad, called Capt'n Tom, had spent much time on Kiawah. In this century farming of the island had been largely abandoned, and the owner, Mr. Adolphus Vanderhorst, gave Capt'n Tom permission to run pigs on the section of Kiawah called Cougar Island and to hunt deer there. Tom and his dad would come out from Charleston in their boat and moor in Bass creek near Willet pond. They really needed a little cabin to store supplies and for the use of the cook whom they would bring along with them. An abandoned horse stable that had been used by the Coast Guard during the first World war was nearby on the eastern end of Otter Island (to the north of Ibis pond). Salvaging the roofing and some timbers from the abandoned stable, they built the cabin in the mid-1940's that we still see today, fifty years later.

Who Wins the Award for Long-distance Flyer? Red Knots, That Visit Us Each Spring and Fall!

In this story, I wish to caution you to respect the needs of one of our shorebirds, but I cannot make that point meaningfully without first telling you what makes this bird so wonderful. And I cannot tell you that until you know which of the shorebirds we are considering. The bird is called the Red knot (*Calidris canutus*), and is a robin-sized bird with a grayish-brown back and whitish breast. In late spring it acquires a reddish cast to the breast as it goes into breeding plumage and thereby probably derives part of its name; the rest, 'knot,' may arise from its subdued *knut* flight call.

Shorebirds are notoriously difficult to distinguish; the knot isn't the tiny gray and white bird that gathers in small flocks of 3 to perhaps 10 and runs ahead of you on the beach with black legs scissoring like wind-up toys—those are Sanderlings. It is not the larger bird we often see singly or in pairs with long beak and long legs that will, when frightened, fly off showing the vibrant black and white wing pattern at each stroke—that is the Willet. No, the Red knot is a gregarious bird and you will find it on the beach in huge flocks of perhaps several hundred. If frightened, they take wing and fly out over the surf wheeling and turning synchronously to display first their white breast surfaces and then the gray of the back—like a marvelously animated cloud.

What makes the Red knot so wonderful, quite aside from the spectacle just described, is the unsurpassed migratory flight that is made each year of its life. They winter as far south as Tierra del Fuego at the tip of South America and nest in the summer on islands in northern Hudson Bay and the high Canadian Arctic; a yearly round-trip flight of about 20,000 miles! They have been known to complete a four-thousand mile leg in sixty hours, and from studies with radar we know that they fly at twenty thousand feet and take advantage of the jet stream to do it. They're truly spectacular migrants!

You might well ask why they make such long migratory trips; the answer is that they move with the changing seasons from one area rich in food to another. This is especially so when they nest in the far north in the summer, for the long period of daylight stimulates the plant life that in turn nurtures the rest of the food chain including great numbers of small clams and crustaceans on the mud flats. This rich food source is essential for the four nestlings each pair usually rears. The other phases of their migration also must match the occurrence of plentiful food supplies, for the long flights consume enormous amounts of energy and each stop must be both for rest and rejuvenation of energy. During these stops, they eat ravenously and may build up fat reserves for the next leg of the journey to the extent that they even double in weight.

Because the Red knots congregate in such vast numbers, they were easy targets for commercial hunters in the last century and great numbers were slaughtered at each migratory flight. In 1916 the Migratory Bird Treaty Act took shorebirds off the game lists and the populations were restored to various degrees. Now however, other human activities threaten them again. It is estimated that one large oil spill in the Delaware Bay, one of the busiest oil-tanker ports in the world and a principle refueling stop for the knots each spring, could disrupt the nesting of a substantial portion of the total American population of the species.

Now for the precaution: when you see the large flocks of Red knots on our beach in spring or again in fall, control your dog and/or children and resist the temptation to put them on the wing even to see once again the beautiful flight patterns. Some of them are feeding ravenously on the small clams in the sand; others are resting on one leg with the other leg and head tucked under a wing. Before they reach the Arctic Circle they will need all the help we can provide.

Please Pull In Those Crab Traps.

Crab traps are no longer allowed in the lagoons on the island, but lagoon manager Norm Shea tells me that he recently had to remove an otter from one. Apparently the otter became entrapped and drowned while trying to reach two spottail bass already in the trap. Quite aside from violating island regulations, people should realize that their crab traps are potential death traps not only for otters but also for diving birds, small alligators or turtles.

Nature's Way of Stabilizing Our Beach.

Mats of brown reeds that may be seen on the beach in the spring serve a valuable function of stabilization. It is true that the mats are rather unsightly for the few weeks that they are seen and they do impede the progress of all, from sun bathers to nesting marine turtles. However, this inconvenience is more than adequately compensated by the large amount of sand retained on the beach by their presence. This is done in two ways. The first and most obvious way as one looks at the beach is that the mats accumulate blown sand and begin the build-up of dunes, and as high tides rise the mats resist the wash out of sand by the retreating waves. The second is less obvious, but if one looks closely at the mats, tiny green spots of new vegetation will be seen. Hence, the mats serve as a mulch and nursery for new vegetation that also stabilizes the beach sand, both by diminishing the force of wind and by resistance of the roots to wash out of sand at high tides.

This is part of a grand cycle that occurs annually. The reed mats originate in the marshes on the other side of the island. Marsh grass (*Spartina alternaflora*) sprouts early in the spring from the roots of the previous growth and rises to heights of 4 to 6 feet. In winter, the grass dies and the dried reeds are washed out of the marsh by high tides the following spring; they are carried to the sea by the Kiawah river, and deposited along our beach by the ocean currents. Thus the physical forces of wind and wave work in concert with plant life to stabilize our island of sand.

SUMMER, 1993

Do Baby Dolphins Get Lost in
The Deep Blue Sea?

One of my concerns on the beach, aside from the turtle nesting program, is keeping a record for the state wildlife department of marine mammals that become stranded. This entails species identification and body measurements. I was struck by the stranding in the fall, both of 1991 and 1992, of young Bottlenose dolphins that apparently were still nursing. In each case the dolphin was only about 45 inches long and with its teeth still encased in the gums. From the small size, each of these calves was very young and possibly even new-born. The thought occurred to me after the second one was found last fall that perhaps dolphins are not very good mothers, and that the calves in both cases had become lost and finally ended up dead upon our shore. Seeking an answer, I found that dolphins are very good mothers indeed, and that some other cause of death of the babies will need to be found. But the story of the first year or so of its life was so interesting that I thought I should share it with you.

When you remember that the dolphin is an air-breathing mammal like ourselves, you can appreciate that the newborn dolphin needs a great deal of help to survive after it is thrust from the warmth of the birth canal into a shockingly cold and suffocating medium. Most are born tail first; so the blowhole is last to emerge, and the laboring mother is normally closely attended by one or more other adults. When the calf emerges, the mother or an attendant may help it to the surface for its first few breaths of air. The calf at birth will weigh as much as 40 pounds and it is this advanced stage of development that permits it to be immediately capable of swimming and shallow diving. Also, the large size probably confers some advantage in minimizing heat loss to the surrounding water. The mother nurses with a pair of teats concealed in slits along the body wall, and the milk, rich in fats, is forcibly ejected by strong muscles surrounding the mammaries. The growth rate is phenomenal and a dolphin calve may double its length and increase its weight by as much as seven fold in the first year. Nevertheless, the calf continues to nurse for a year or more and is closely attended by adults during that time. "Babysitting" has been observed, in which other adults of the pod remain with a calf as its mother forages for food. As the calf matures, it becomes more independent, tastes scraps of food in the wake of feeding adults and gradually learns to hunt.

Echolocation is a peculiar ability that dolphins and whales share with the bat. Unlike the bat, Bottlenose dolphins do not depend by necessity upon echolocation, for they have keen vision in water as well as through the water-air interface. This is shown by their ability to track and capture airborne flying fish and perform all the tricks of Flipper. However, in turbid water or in poor light, their echolocation ability is of tremendous advantage in locating prey. They produce whistling sounds and series of short clicks at high frequencies; in fact their echo direction-finding system seems to surpass in quality that of the bat. In murky waters and with their eyes covered, they effortlessly find their prey and can even distinguish dead fish from water-filled gelatin dummies. Perhaps the amount of time required to learn these and other feeding-related skills necessitates the long period of dependency of the calf upon mother and the "babysitters."

The two babies that I found on the beach may have been still-born or perhaps died of some disease shortly after birth, for the mortality rate of about 20 percent is highest in the first year of their life, and pneumonia is a common contributor to infant death. Whatever the cause of death, the loss was not a mere statistic in some wildlife department file, but was a tragic event in the dolphin community. Losing an infant appears to be very stressful for the mother. Numerous reports, both from oceanariums and from the wild, describe mothers supporting dead calves at the surface, sometimes for days.

The Protective Program for Loggerhead Turtle Nesting on Kiawah Island Goes Volunteer.

You may recall that in Winter, 1992 I related the early history of efforts to protect turtle nests on the beach. By the close of the 1987 season, it seemed that the program might be discontinued. However, this story will tell of its rescue.

1988

Well, before the nesting season, it was obvious that the protective program would not be operating. Buzz Botts, who had operated the program the year before, had moved to Savannah and the beach gates were locked; no access was permitted. I went to Fort Johnson for a two-hour mini-course in turtle nest management from Sally Murphy, the wildlife agent in charge of marine turtle protection for the South Carolina coast. Returning with a permit to conduct the program, I did some arm twisting and came up with nine other "volunteers." However, it was not until the Fourth of July that I was able to obtain a key to the locked gate, thus half the season was lost.

Our approach was simplistic, and our objectives were two: obtain a count of nesting crawls for the remainder of the season, and keep a record of strandings (dead turtles) on the beach. Because many of the flags that marked the nests were removed or difficult to relocate, no attempt was made to determine hatching success. However, a report was written and recommendations for the following year were made. We hoped to recruit more volunteers, find financial support, begin a public awareness program and do a better job on the beach.

1989

The 1989 season began well. We persuaded the Community Association to provide a budget of $1600 for the program. In addition, we obtained the loan of a 4-wheel drive vehicle from Security for the summer. The vehicle, good old #510 to some, something less flattering for others, had seen better days and been subjected to too many uncaring drivers. The first thing all learned was never, never put on the emergency brake—otherwise a mechanic would be needed to free it. There were other minor peculiarities; often it refused to go into reverse; and always it refused to stay in 4-wheel drive unless the co-pilot held the shift in that position. With the season assured by all this material support we sought volunteers and our list jumped from the 10 of the previous year to 24 for 1989. Truly we felt that we had passed from the Dark Ages to the Renaissance (I sure hope no historian ever reads this!)

Ruth Cusick attended the briefing session at Ft. Johnson so we would have two "experts" and as a first move toward diversification of responsibility, a committee of Bill Connellee, Ruth and me was formed to run the program for the season. After the nesting terminated on August 13th, hatching patrols were made weekly to inspect nests, record hatchings and monitor raccoon predation. I had scheduled a little party on September 28th for our volunteers to celebrate a good season, but Hurricane Hugo had other plans as it roared ashore on September 21st. Fortunately the hurricane did no harm to our beach so the turtles still in their nests remained undisturbed. In conclusion,

1989 was a learning year for all of us, and we felt optimistically that we could do a better job in 1990.

1990

This year we had the heady experience of being offered sponsorship by *two* organizations, the Community Association and the new Town of Kiawah Island. We chose to go with the town and have not regretted it. The town agreed to support the program with a budget of $2500 from Accommodation Tax funds. Through the efforts of George Spaulding, a pickup truck was loaned to the program for the summer by the John Parker automobile dealership in Charleston. Our volunteers increased to 34 and everything looked fine.

Up to this time, our objectives had been to catalog the number and location of nests, relocate some, and protect all as best we could. This comes under the heading of protection of the rookery and will always be the primary objective. However, we now felt sufficiently advanced to be able to share our experience and knowledge with others and so we took on a second objective of public education. We began a series of slide shows each Monday evening at the East Beach Conference Center. Bill Connellee collaborated with the Recreation Department of the Landmark organization in arranging the talks and gave most of the presentations.

An amusing event in the midst of the season was the turtle that became disoriented and ended up touring the Ryder Cup golf course that was then under construction. In the morning we could see her track weaving over sand dunes that looked like a movie set for the Sahara desert. We tracked her to the large lagoon between what are now the 15th and 16th holes. She showed no inclination to come out except to lay her eggs on the "fairway" after a few days. The course designer, Pete Dye, and I relocated the nest on the beach, but early attempts by Sally Murphy and other staff of the state Wildlife & Marine Resources Dept. failed to catch her. A similar situation had occurred a few years earlier at Fripp Island, and that turtle, who acquired the name Tootsie, was not returned to the ocean until she was rendered sluggish by cold weather in the late fall. Our turtle received the name Tootsie Too, and she remained in the lagoon until a full-scale attack by scuba divers in the fall drove her into a net. Then back to the ocean she rode in the back of a pick-up truck.

Hatching was monitored extensively and nest success was 77%, which was good in consideration of the total destruction of 18 nests by raccoons and partial destruction of 20 others. A brief attempt was made to remove raccoons by trapping. The animals were easily caught, but trapping was terminated after five had been taken, because of the unhappiness of some volunteers and the realization that very large numbers would need to be removed in order to be effective. The 1990 season ended on October 12th; heavy rains soaked the beach and high tides pushed up the beach by strong off-shore winds flooded the last three nests. If the storm had occurred a month earlier, the loss of nests would have been catastrophic. This illustrates that success of the rookery is not totally in the hands of man; there are threats beyond our control and against which our efforts are futile.

1991

The town purchased a new pickup truck for our program—it was so beautiful we were almost afraid to take it out on the beach! Predation by raccoons at the beginning of the season was heavy and foxes too were raiding on a significant scale. The use of larger screens, plus the installation of an electrified fence at nests already partially destroyed drastically decreased the predation. There was exceptionally heavy rainfall in the summer of 1991 which promoted heavy vegetation of the foredunes, and the nest success rate was down to 49% as compared to 77% the previous year. More and more the fact is thrust upon us that our beach is not static and that we will always need to be vigilant to counteract changes and the problems they create.

This year marked the beginning of a new undertaking. We began special studies of problems of the kind just mentioned and others directed toward increasing our general knowledge of the Loggerhead turtle as a species. This then became a fourth major aspect of the program in addition to the earlier ones of 1) protection of nests, 2) accumulation of comprehensive data, and 3) public education. These special studies not only add value to the program but also provide stimulating interest for some of the volunteers. Three of these studies were reported in the 1991 annual report: design of electrified fencing to repel predators; determination of the water table at spring tides; and identification of dune plants capable of extending roots into nests. (The results on electrified fencing were reported at the 1992 Workshop on Sea Turtle Biology and Conservation at Jekyll Island, Ga.) A party to celebrate the year was held at the property-owners pool, and this time no storm intruded to mar a happy evening.

1992

The 1992 season began with continued support by the Town of Kiawah Island, and our volunteer staff had by now increased to 79 members. In continuation of my efforts to diffuse responsibility and increase the sense of participation, the operating committee was increased to five by the return of Ruth Cusick and the addition of Jack Hamilton as a new member. Further, the nest patrol period was divided between three teams, each of which operated independently, although under the same general guidelines. A fourth team run by George and Kay Walther monitored the hatching and the post-hatching evaluation.

Public relations were strongly emphasized both with the formal lectures and the many discussions with interested people on the beach. Favorable publicity of our program, although not aggressively promoted, has occurred over the years with articles in the Charleston newspaper, the local Islands magazine, several travel magazines, and for the past three years on one or another of the local TV stations.

Research studies continued in several areas. The study of changes in the water table at various tide levels was continued from last year. A new study was begun on the temperature within the nest during the incubation period, relative to the changes in beach temperature from May through October. These temperature studies are pertinent both for the length of the incubation period and for the sex ratio of the hatchlings. Finally, a very exploratory study was begun on the feasibility of identifying the nesting turtle by the unique pattern of crawl marks. This year, the study was limited to accumulation of photographs of various crawls and an attempt to classify patterns.

As often happens, a nesting turtle provided exciting moments this year. In this instance, the turtle chose to make her nest beside the steps of a busy boardwalk on a night that just happened to be the 4th of July. In response to a rather urgent call from Security, I arrived about 9:30 PM. The noisy spectators shone flashlights on her as they moved up and down the stairs; the fireworks display had just begun; but she seemed unperturbed as the rockets flashed and boomed above. Of course, it was tough on all the children clustered around. They just couldn't watch her and the fireworks at the same time.

When the fireworks ended in the grand finale and the beach subsided into darkness and quiet, she labored on. By now she had been excavating the nest for over an hour, the children were impatient, and the mothers were anxious to tuck them into bed. What was the problem? Shining my flashlight at the construction site, I saw that most of her left rear flipper was missing. Probably a shark had taken it earlier in her life. This was a dilemma, and by the looks I received from the audience, I was expected to solve it. Remembering the story of a similar incident related to me by Charlotte Hope of the state wildlife department, I lay prone on the sand behind the turtle and prepared to play the role of midwife. After all, I had been delivering baby turtles from their nests for years; therefore, I felt quite qualified. Each time the left flipper came up empty of sand, I thrust my arm down and scooped up sand before the right flipper came down for its load. Between the two of us, we soon had an acceptable nest.

The turtle gave a sigh of relief, I gave an even bigger sigh of relief, and all the   children applauded *sotto voce* as the eggs began to emerge. After those brave enough had touched a moist egg fresh from the delivery, they were all hustled off by the relieved mothers, and the turtle and I were left alone in the darkness. She closed the nest quite skillfully and departed into the surf without so much as a backward glance at her benefactor. Whew! Time for a late shower and bed.*

If You Think A Bird Is Laughing at You, You're Not Paranoid, It's Just Our Laughing Gull.

Our most common summer gull, the one with the jet black head, is often   heard emitting a raucous cackle as though it knew a secret joke and couldn't wait to tell the other gulls. Yes, the Laughing gulls are well named. They arrive in the spring and quickly begin their   courtship and pairing for the nesting season soon to come in May. Locally, most of their nests are on Bird Key in the Stono river at the east end of the island. They share nesting sites with the Brown pelicans and Royal terns, and all seem to get along fairly amiably. Their simple nests are located in the dense tufts of grasses that grow on the tiny island, and often their colony may number in the hundreds.

The chicks remain in the nest for about a week, and in a summer as hot as the current one they are susceptible to dehydration and heat exhaustion. The parents take turns shading the nest with their bodies, and in addition bring water to cool the chicks. You may see this behavior in the middle of a hot day as the gulls fly to a shallow pool of fresh water on Kiawah. They wade in, settle down to soak their breast feathers, then off they fly, directly back toward   Bird Key and their panting chicks. As the chicks develop, they leave the nest and soon are scurrying about the colony and hiding beneath vegetation to avoid predators as well as the sun.

If this series of chapters on turtle nesting has struck a responsive chord in your bosom, we always welcome new volunteers and can find a place for you in the program. I promise that you will not be required to perform midwife duties.

The question might be asked how the parents distinguish their young from the other chicks all over the nesting colony. The answer seems to be that the chicks quickly learn to recognize the call of their parents and the parents in turn distinguish their chick by its quick response to their call. Typically, the chick rushes up and begs for the tiny fish brought by its parents. Later in the summer, the juvenile birds join the adults on the beach and are distinguishable from the adults in the flock by the mottled tan plumage on the head in contrast to the black of the adults.

Laughing gulls are omnivorous and far from finicky eaters; they can be seen on occasion behaving like fly-catchers as they pass through swarms of insects and catch them in mid- air. At other times, they may be seen flying in small flocks over the marsh at low tide and diving down for a Fiddler crab snatched from the crowds that roam the mud flats. However, their most amusing feeding habit is the robbing of pelicans of their catch. When a pelican rises to the surface with a pouch full of small fry, one or another of the gulls attempts and often succeeds in lighting on the pelican's head and helping itself to the bountiful supply in the capacious pouch. Other gulls hover about and pick up the scraps that fall in the water.

Later in the fall our Laughing gulls desert us for warmer spots in Georgia and Florida where foods are more plentiful. But they will return again, cackling over new stories about the amusing plumage seen on those tourists south of the border.

In the Fall, Belligerent Bucks
Have the Right of Way.

At this time of year buck deer change from shy creatures of the forest to aggressive males whose behavior is often unpredictable. The reason is hormonal changes in the animals at the season of "rut." This is the climax of a series of changes, most of them triggered by alterations in hormonal levels, that occur in both male and female deer as they prepare for the annual mating season. In early spring the bucks began to form a new set of antlers to replace the ones cast off during the winter. Antler development is set in motion in response to changes in the number of daylight hours, in this case the increased day length with the coming of spring. These bony structures are initially sheathed in a soft skin called velvet and grow quite rapidly (sometimes as much as one or two inches in a week.) As day length shortens in August and September, hormonal levels of testosterone increase and the antlers begin to harden. The mineralization of the antlers stimulates the bucks to vigorously rub their antlers on bushes or small trees to remove the velvet, much to the dismay of the home-owner who views the broken branches on his favorite shrub.

At this stage the antlers have been converted into formidable weapons for the buck in its contests with other bucks for possession of a territory that may amount to several square miles and the opportunities to mate with the females as they come into estrus. You may see evidence of these contests as scuffed-up marks in your yard or even hear the rattling of the antlers as the bucks joust in the night. Sometimes this bellicose mood is so powerful that the buck challenges other animals and even humans. If you encounter a large buck standing erect, staring at you and perhaps even pawing the ground with his fore-hooves, don't accept the challenge. A retreat is the prudent course. In any event do not advance toward him with the idea of calling his bluff; an unarmed man is certain to lose that contest. Especially dangerous is the buck that has lost his fear of humans, possibly by being feed over a period of time in someone's backyard.

When all the fighting and breeding is over, bucks shed their antlers and settled down to a more sociable and quieter life. They band together with does and fawns to face the winter together. But then, the lengthening days of spring will drive them to repeat the entire cycle once again.

Bird Feeders and Baths.

Many people will note a significant drop-off in the number of birds coming to their feeders at this time of year and they may wonder why the birds have deserted them. Natural foods are most abundant in the fall, so the birds don't need us now. If you inspect the vines and shrubs along almost any natural edging, whether in the dunes, along the roadway, at the marsh edge or the borders of any vacant lot, you will see that they are loaded with berries, seeds and other nutritious fruits. Be prompt in your inspection, however, for the birds and other animals are foraging vigorously and these foods are disappearing rapidly. The birds will need us later when these natural food sources are exhausted, so keep the feeders filled.

Hummingbird feeders left out past the birds' normal migration period will not encourage the birds to linger beyond their normal departure time. Most hummingbirds will leave by mid-October whether the feeders are out or not. Migration instincts are related more to length of daylight than to feeding habits. They are greatly attracted to the cannas in my yard and the entire family will be swirling about the blooms even in October and then, suddenly one day, they are gone.

What birds need most of all at this season is water. If you keep a well-placed bird bath clean and filled, the birds will show their appreciation by using it all year long. Yes, they will even enjoy a good bath on a sunny day in winter! Location of the bath should take a bit of thought. They seem to prefer to have it located on the ground but it will be safer for the birds on a pedestal. Location in full sun places the birds in too vulnerable a position for predators, whether it be the neighborhood cat or the passing hawk. Also, it will become too hot and overgrown with algae in summer. A more secluded and fairly shady place is better, preferably with overhead branches for drying and preening, but not close to bushes where the cat can lurk. The bath should slope from 1 to 2 inches deep and have a roughened surface to prevent slippage. If you can rig up a way to drip water into the bath, you will attract a lot more birds. The sound is like a magnet for birds and may bring some rarer ones, such as warblers and flycatchers that would not visit your feeder.

To the Plant Community, Our Dunes Are A Desert.

I had the good fortune to wander over a portion of the Great Basin desert in Utah not long ago and encountered a number of old friends that I know from our Kiawah dunes. Yes, some of the same plants or their close relatives are able to survive in the desert. When you think about it that is not too surprising, because similar harsh conditions prevail in both places. Most vegetation must compete for sun and space but these plants of the desert and the dunes compete mainly for water, and the ones that survive must be able to cope with full sun, strong winds, unstable soil, uncertain rainfall and high salinity. Only plants that have developed unusual defenses could exist in either place, and perhaps we can consider those ingenious defensive measures later.

One of the best known of these plants is the infamous Russian thistle which is the source of the "Tumblin' Tumbleweed" of western ballad fame and is universally loathed all the way from our turtle nesting patrol people to the ranchers of the southwest. Because it is so widespread, it may come as a surprise to learn that it is an alien—and a subversive one at that. The first seeds are believed to have arrived in a shipment of flax seeds from Russia to North Dakota in 1873, and apparently it found our wastelands as agreeable as the bleak and wind-blown steppes of Mother Russia.

This annual appears on our beach in late spring as serrated purplish green spikes pushing up through the sand. By mid summer the minute leaves harden and sharpen into an impenetrable armor of short thorns. Tiny white flowers, each with a tinier blood- drop in the center, nestle in the protection of the thorns. Despite the space between plants in the dunes, intense competition exists and the thistle is the starling of the plant community. So, when it breaks free from its roots and bounces along the desert (or our beach), scattering those thousands of seeds for perpetuation of the species I can just hear the rustle of leaves as all the other plants shudder and mummer,"There goes the neighborhood!"

Cougar, Is That Really You?

"Softly, like a whisper in the night, it creeps in and out of our Southern psyche. It's the stuff legends are made of. Elusive and mysterious, the graceful eastern cougar has existed more in our minds, imaginations, tales and fables than in reality. Or has it?"

This is the way an article on the cougar was begun by Pris Massenburg of the Nongame and Heritage Trust of our state wildlife department. An animal of the western hemisphere, the cougar was one of the first New World animals recorded by explorers, and was common throughout the continental United States. It is still fairly common in the West, but in the East it now is known to exist only in southern Florida, although it could exist almost anywhere that offers sufficient prey and adequate cover. Its food of choice is deer, but it will settle for squirrels, raccoons, wild pigs and other small mammals. This nocturnal cat has no specific den except during breeding season, and is a restless animal. It may travel up to 20 miles in a night, and may range over as much as 150,000 acres (about 15 times the total acreage of Kiawah Island).

Cougars are so secretive, so rare and wander over an area so great that the chances of seeing one are slim even if it does pass through the island. If you happen to see an animal with a long tawny buff or reddish brown body, a creamy white belly, a long dark-tipped tail and small head with rounded ears, then indeed you might be seeing a cougar. An adult can attain a length of 7 feet, including a tail extending perhaps 3-4 feet. It may weigh as much as 120-150 pounds, although a smaller size of half that weight is quite possible. (By comparison, our Bobcat has a body length of 3 feet and weight of only 20 pounds.)

Despite the poor odds of seeing this cat, the wildlife department does get reported sightings each year and I frequently receive reports of sightings on Kiawah. An example of a reliable report was one made to the wildlife department several years ago by Talmadge Lewis. I first met Tal when he was the architect for our first home on the island but most of you may recognize him as a wildlife photographer who has exhibited frequently in the Charleston area. Let him relate the event,

> "My wife and I were returning home to Kiawah Island when it ran across the road in front of the jeep just after we turned off Maybank Highway onto Berry Hill Road, a short-cut to Kiawah. The cat weighed about 50 to 60 pounds. The body was slender with a long tail, and was a dark tawny color."

Because Tal has photographed cougars in southern Florida, he feels confident in his ability to distinguish a cougar from a bobcat or other feline. However, he adds that he wouldn't bet his life that the John's Island animal was a cougar.

So the mystery remains, and how will we ever put the matter to rest? Wildlife personnel inform me that only a photograph, a paw print or a scat (feces) will be acceptable evidence, short of a roadkill. A good photograph will be great if we can only arrange an appointment between the cat and the photographer with his paraphernalia in place and the sun shining brightly. In lieu of that, a paw print would be nice but the animal typically walks on logs, meanders back and forth along the edge of roads and avoids wet or muddy spots. Why would a collection of scat be acceptable? Like most cats, cougars groom themselves frequently by licking their fur. The loose hair is ingested and passes out in the feces, and the modern analytical laboratory can readily distinguish hair of that species, the long awaited cougar.

So, I can do no better than again quote Pris Massenberg, *"A solitary animal, so secretive and silent afoot, does it walk among us like a ghost in the night?"*

Another Successful Turtle Nesting Season.

All of the nests have hatched and the last hatchlings were put to sea in October, to the great relief of the hardworking crew that kept the vigil. The number of 96 nests was quite low, for the average is nearly 150 nests. However, the 87 volunteers on the nesting and hatching patrols more than made up for that low number by putting 5,220 hatchlings into the ocean. This amounts to 54.4 hatchlings per nest; the highest number previous to this was the 10.8 hatchlings per nest last year.

This spectacular increase is attributable to the experience of the relocation and hatching crews, and to the relocation of most nests which circumvented losses to flooding and root invasion that were such problems in previous years. Three volunteers, Joanne Barrand, Jane Smith and Joan Wassen practically lived on the beach during the hatching season, and rumor has it that the Great Mother Turtle who lives at the bottom of the sea will award each of these ladies the coveted golden medallion with crossed flippers.

An innovation this year was the photographing of the pattern of marks made by each female turtle as she crawled up the beach to make her nest. It is hoped that the pattern will prove to be unique for each turtle and will permit us to determine the number and nesting behavior of the turtles using the Kiawah rookery. This year it appears that only 23 turtles nested here with an average of 4.0 nests/turtle. This low number of nesting turtles has especial significance when it is realized that 11 turtles washed ashore dead this past summer!

Sometimes A Luncheon Guest Becomes the Entrée

It was the day before Thanksgiving, a delightfully warm and sunny day in the prolonged Indian Summer that we call fall on Kiawah. I had just gone in to prepare my lunch when through the open window I heard the raucous squawks that only a Great Blue heron is capable of emitting. I thought nothing of it, because a Great Blue spends a lot of time on our bank bordering on Canvasback pond. It appreciates the dead tree snag that runs out into the pond and serves admirably as a fishing stand, and protests loudly when disturbed. These were not the usual calls, however, for they conveyed a desperate note and ran on far too long. Dashing out onto the deck, I observed the heron half submerged in the pond about 15 feet from its fishing perch. Its huge gray wings were flailing the surface of the pond and the long, sharp beak was stabbing frantically at something beneath the water. As I stood there in shocked disbelief, it freed itself, leaped into the air, and flapped rather erratically to the opposite bank. It was able to stand firmly on two legs, to my great relief, for by now I realized that the trap beneath the waves had been set by one of our alligators in search of lunch.

The menu was more varied than either the alligator or I had expected, because almost immediately after the departure of the heron two Anhingas surfaced at the same spot. They too had apparently been cruising beneath the surface for lunch and curiosity had drawn them to the commotion I had just wit-

nessed. Almost immediately the two dark birds began to swirl about one another with wings flapping and beaks jabbing at each other—most extraordinary behavior. One disappeared beneath the surface, not in the typical graceful surface dive but an abrupt vertical plunge like a fisherman's bobbing cork at the moment of the big strike, and the second paddled off at full speed.

Immediately, the pond returned to its normal benign appearance with sun beams dancing on the wavelets and the tiny birds carrying on their twittering conversations; no trace remained of the drama played out in the brief span of perhaps two minutes. I wished the alligator 'bon apetit' and returned sadly to my own luncheon preparations. But as I did so I glanced across the pond to the heron still watching all of this. I wondered what was going through its mind and whether it would ever again return to its favorite fishing perch.

Bufflehead Pond Nature Area

A decade ago Bufflehead was a secluded pond with a nicely balanced community of wildlife, but even then it was undergoing changes. These changes are normal for shallow ponds; as aquatic vegetation proliferates annually, the debris accumulates to render the pond ever shallower, and bushes and trees such as wax myrtle and palmetto advance farther into the pond from the perimeter. If the succession were allowed to proceed unimpeded, a stand of palmettos and wax myrtles would cover the original pond site. To reverse this process, the pond must be deepened. For several years this expensive undertaking was sidestepped and various alternatives that included ditching and herbiciding were tried. These only added to the unsightliness of the poor pond. Finally, the developer came to the rescue, and excavation of the pond was started in November.

However, the history of Bufflehead pond may be more intriguing than just described. A hint that this was so arose when I had the opportunity to discuss the pond with Gary Otter who was in charge of the restoration. When Gary turned off the controls of the mammoth dredge and climbed down from the cab to where I was standing in the muck beside the huge treads, I had the opportunity to discuss the operation with him. I quickly realized that the pond meant more to Gary than just another contract, for he obviously was interested in the wildlife and the possible benefits that might accrue from the restoration.

For example, he plans to carefully remove the dead cedar trees that now border the pond and add so much interest as their bleached limbs extend outward and upward from the pond surface. After grading the bottom of the pond, he will reposition the cedars somewhat further out from shore than at present so that water birds will feel more secure perching on them. Another thing that Gary mentioned was that in the course of dredging he had pulled from the center of the pond the residual roots of large pines (probably of the Loblolly species) and trunks of palmettos. Because the pines could not grow in the wet soil of the pond, it suggests that at some time in the past the area was much drier. Numerous explanations might be proposed but clearly the occurrence of these trees sometime in the past suggests that the pond area has undergone more than one successional change.

Now, it will be up to Norman Shea, as lagoon manager for the Community Association, to maintain the proper water level and re-introduce desirable aquatic plants that flourish in brackish water. These probably will include some for protective cover such as the tall marsh grass (*Spartina alternaflora*), and others as food sources such as salt marsh bulrush (*Scriptus robustus*), and the submersed widgeon grass (*Ruppia maritima*). It will not be an easy undertaking for Norm to achieve complete rehabilitation, because he must balance the aesthetic demands of people and the needs of wildlife. With time, the animals and birds will give us their answer by their presence or absence from the pond. Whatever their response may be, it will be interesting for us all to follow this commendable attempt toward restoration.

If You Eat Like A Bird, You Are A Glutton.

Birds, like all animals, must eat to live, and if we analyze what most birds do during an average day, we would be justified to conclude that they live to eat. Only the rituals of the breeding cycle even begin to claim a bird's time and attention to the degree that feeding activities do. Depending as we now do on supermarkets and restaurants, most of us forget that such an all-consuming obsession with procuring food is the norm in the animal kingdom, including most humans in hunter-gatherer cultures. To most of us a meal is an event that occurs rather briefly each day at set times. To a bird, however, the urge to feed is a drive that is nearly continuous; it is more a normal function, like breathing, than separate events in the day.

The Birder's Handbook by Paul R. Ehrlich (Simon & Schuster Inc., 1988) contains many interesting observations about the food requirements of birds, and I have incorporated a number of these here. In general, the smaller the bird, the more it eats in proportion to its body weight. This is because a small bird has a larger surface (through which heat is lost) in relation to its mass than does a larger bird. For example, an eagle may eat 2 pounds of meat a day and a pelican 4 pounds of fish, and these amounts constitute about a quarter of the body weight. By contrast, a hummingbird may consume only half an ounce of nectar and insects in a day, but that still amounts to twice its body weight. With their tiny bodies and high levels of activity, hummingbirds have the highest metabolic rates of all animals.

Theoretically, it can be calculated that a warm blooded animal cannot be smaller than a hummingbird or a shrew; further reduction in size would make it impossible for the creature to eat fast enough to maintain its body temperature. Indeed, some hummingbirds conserve energy by becoming torpid at night; that is, they let their body temperature drop, often until it is close to that of the surrounding air. So we must say goodbye to them until next spring. Other small birds that winter here such as chickadees and titmice also are stressed by cold weather, and they must eat continuously during the brief daylight hours. If they did not, they also would not possess enough fuel to see then through the long, cold night. Lynne Langley, in one of her delightful Nature Watch columns for the Post and Courier newspaper, relates that some seed eaters have devised another means of stoking the metabolic fires through the night. The bird has a crop in the esophagus and packs it with seed just before dark; once asleep, it slowly digests the seeds that provide the energy to maintain its body temperature.

In part, the driving force in the continual search for food is the restricted diet of the specific species. Some birds such as the crow and the blackbird are omnivorous, that is, they will eat about anything they capture. Most birds are much more selective; consequently, they normally ignore many potential food sources in search of the customary one which may be present in limited amount. It is only when these foods are insufficient because of the stress of cold weather that birds turn avidly to the high caloric suet and peanut butter that some of us put out at this time of the year.

Cormorants and Pelicans on the Ponds in Winter

Double-crested cormorants and Brown pelicans normally are not considered among the birds that are stressed by the winter cold. However, Kiawah Island is in the coastal region where these two species remain in the winter, and yet where the water temperature falls to a point that renders ocean fish unavailable. Both species must turn from the ocean, usually in December, as the surface water of the sea turns cold and the small fish retreat to warmer water deeper down on the continental shelf. Then, they come to the ponds of Kiawah for fish to maintain them until the inshore water of the ocean warms enough for the ocean fish to return in the spring. On the ponds, the cormorant seems to feel most at home for it can continue its normal feeding behavior of surface diving, and pursuing fish as it swiftly propels itself forward by its powerful webbed feet. Rising to the surface after perhaps 15-20 seconds, and vigorously shaking its head to send a crescent shower of glistening droplets spinning outward, it displays its success as it deftly maneuvers a small fish in its bill for a quick swallow head first.

The pelican, however, appears sadly out of place and even takes on a doleful expression as though it knew it looked ridiculous on the tiny pond. Usually it does not attempt aerial dives to capture fish, because that would be dangerous due to the turbidity of the water and the shallowness of most ponds. Instead, it resorts to floating on the surface and snatching at the fish that incautiously swim near. Unlike the cormorant, it is not built for swimming beneath the water and its eyes are not adapted for underwater vision. However, surface fishing by the Brown pelican is not an extreme departure from normal pelican behavior, for its close cousin, the White pelican, normally floats about and catches fish from the surface. The pelicans are frequently seen on the same pond as the cormorants, and they keep close to the cormorants who are likely, in turn, to be close to a school of fish. From time to time, one species may be seen trying to rob the other of its fish, but generally they get along well together, and continue the close association that they display in warmer weather as they rest together on sand bars.

The Abundant Waterfowl on Pintail Pond

Those of you that enjoy viewing waterfowl on the ponds should keep an eye on Pintail Pond, for it seems to attract a greater number and variety of species than other ponds. Pintail is the long pond that runs along the first and ninth holes of Osprey golf course, and access is available to non-golfers only in the early morning and late evening when the pond is at its loveliest and the birds are most numerous.

At the time the golf course was created, the shallow pond was excavated with a six to ten foot trench around the perimeter leaving low-lying islands in the center. This change was designed to provide a hospitable habitat both for fish and waterfowl, and it has been quite successful. Today it has a vigorous growth of aquatic plants around the periphery as well as on the central islands, and is a favorite for both waterfowl and alligators that seem to maintain a cautious truce (most of the time!).

I inspected the pond early on New Year's Day, and came up with the following tally:

3	Great Blue herons	1	Tricolor heron
3	Common egrets	9	Black-crowned Night herons
1	Snowy egret	2	Anhingas
11	Brown pelicans	48	Double-crested cormorants
21	Common gallinules	3	Pied-billed grebes
6	Green-winged teals	2	Coots

In addition to these waterfowl, there were other birds hopping and flying about. For example, four Bluebirds were fluffed up and showing their colorful plumage to good effect as they perched on tall stems of dead grasses and darted with flashes of blue to the sere fairway for the insects that somehow had the energy despite the cold to move about and reveal themselves to these sharp-eyed birds. They were traveling along with a flock of Yellow-rumped warblers which are the most numerous of the smaller birds on the island in the winter. You do not need to be an expert birder to recognize the Yellow-rump warbler for its name gives it away. The sparrow-sized birds are easily identified as they flit about by the distinctive bright yellow patch on the rump as prominent as a signal light. As we move into the spring season, both the numbers and species of waterfowl will change as some move up north for the summer and others come in from their winter vacations to the south. As you golfers pass over the bridge toward the second hole, watch for these changes.

Other Bird Sightings

Stan Novaco had the rare experience of seeing a Peregrine falcon alight momentarily in a planter at his home. The sighting was especially meaningful for Stan because he had been involved in a conservation program for the species in Detroit.

An adult Bald eagle was seen by a number of people on the island this winter. Perhaps the best sighting was by David Sullivan who had the thrill of seeing it scoop up a fish from the lagoon in back of his home.

The migratory flocks of American robins were moving through in great numbers early in February and banging against our windows—don't they encounter windows where they usually dwell?

A pair of Great Horned owls is nesting here again this winter. Hint: the pair is using an Osprey nest, but not the same one as the winter before. Details will follow.

When A Whale Comes to Kiawah.

One day late in February, Carl and Margit Obern telephoned with some excitement to say that they had been out on the beach for a bit of sun and encountered a dead whale. These unusual events are always exciting so I quickly joined them on the beach in front of the Ocean Course clubhouse. As I followed my friends' little blue jeep the 1½ miles to the eastern tip of the island, I wondered why they needed to travel so far for a patch of sun on Kiawah. However, I was glad that they had for it gave us the opportunity to claim discovery of the whale before the crew of the Coastguard helicopter.

The sandbar over which we traveled is exposed only at low tide, and it changes size and shape almost weekly. Its immensity gave me the feeling of moving over the back of a great tan whale with the water of the ocean on one side, water of a tidal slough on the other, and the only sense of land being the trees marking the Ocean course about half a mile inland. Eventually I espied the whale as a tiny black dot in the distance, and as we approached, it took on the dimensions of one of the smaller whales. Even in death it was impressive. Its sleek shape and smooth licorice-black skin made it look as though it had just been extruded from a plastic press; the under-slung jaw with its incurved teeth, the bulbous forehead and sickle-shaped lateral fins gave it a predatory cast.

After much measuring, counting of teeth and noting of shape, size and positioning of fins, we decided that it corresponded to the Short-finned pilot whale in my guidebook. The only other whale stranding on Kiawah that I am aware of occurred in the 1960's, for George and Lib Melvin told me that there was a mass stranding of 25 or 30 pilot whales at the eastern end of the island. This pelagic species seldom comes into shallow coastal waters, and the cause of these mass strandings remains a mystery. However, the whale we had just viewed was not the forerunner of such an event, because its physical condition would suggest that it must have died in the ocean and drifted for a number of days before washing shore.

The sequel came the next day just before low tide as the three of us again assembled at the whale, but now we were reinforced by three men and a woman from the Charleston laboratory of NOAA/NMFS (National Oceanic and Atmospheric Administration/National Marine Fishery Service). The young crew was lead by Wayne McFee, and we quickly realized that they were determined to extract every bit of information possible from this rare find. They worked quickly for the next two hours to beat the incoming tide, and took every conceivable measurement from total length of just under 12 feet to size of eye, blow hole, to say nothing of the genital slit. As teeth were counted, I noted that they were so widely spaced that they did not seem very effective until I remembered that the principal prey is soft-bodied squid. I visualized the whale pursuing squid in the dark depths as I inspected the bulging forehead, called the melon, that sent out the sonic signals essential for successful pursuit of prey in that total darkness. After all the probing and measuring, they determined that the whale was an adult male, and possible an old one, because the teeth were worn and some were missing. Because the skin was unblemished except for sucker disc marks from the squid, the cause of death could not be determined.

Then they sharpened knives and fitted scalpel blades to begin the difficult task of removing portions of the animal of special scientific interest. All of us were thankful that a brisk breeze was blowing during all this time and I noted that spectators as well as workers positioned themselves on the windward side. The head was of greatest value and the most difficult to detach as can be imagined, but after much sawing and resharpening of knives it was removed, and a necessarily rather crude dissection continued. Wayne exposed the inner ear and extracted threadlike nematodes that are frequently found and may affect the equilibrium of the animal.

Other tidbits were brought up for my inspection, the most notable being an eyeball about the size of a billiard ball. As it was casually tossed on the mounting pile of refuse, I thought of all the visions that had passed through that eye during the many years of the animal's lifetime; visions that are beyond the imagination of we terrestrial beings. Finally, the head was bagged for further treatment in the laboratory to yield the white skull that would end up on exhibition in some museum, classroom or agency office.

Another skeletal feature of great interest was the state of fusion of some of the vertebrae. The cervical vertebrae near the head fuse, but others farther down the spinal column that normally are unfused may grow together, perhaps through an arthritic condition. This would lead to rigidity of the spine just where the whale needs the flexibility to drive the tail for propulsion. After a great deal of vigorous effort and much care not to penetrate the body cavities which might produce a volcanic explosion that workers and spectators alike would have deeply regretted, one vertebra was extracted for later study.

By now the entire crew was worn out from their efforts; the tide was rising, and a change of weather was signaled by dark clouds moving over from Seabrook, a distinct drop in temperature and an increase in wind velocity. All were happy to call it quits, and unwanted pieces from the dissection were tossed into a pit that Carl dug with a turtle patrol shovel from my truck.

As I drove past the poor carcass, missing its head, one pectoral fin and other vital parts, it no longer resembled a whale. I still retained my admiration for the dedication of the young crew that labored so hard to extract all the information they could from this animal that was fated to be torn apart and consumed some where in some way. And yet, my strongest feeling was one of regret that such a magnificent animal should end up butchered on alien terrain. How much better for it to have settled to the bottom of the ocean for final disposal bv others of its realm.

SPRING, 1994

The Valuable Marshlands of Kiawah

The marsh is one of the great resources of Kiawah Island, and the equal of the beach in importance. Off-shore sandbars, the beach and dunes all stabilize the island by buffering it against storms and ocean currents. In similar fashion, the wide marsh with its tall grass protects the island by buffering it against erosion from river currents and the high winds and surge-waves that accompany storms such as hurricane Hugo.

The grass stands virtually as a monoculture of *Spartina alternaflora*, commonly referred to as spartina or cordgrass. In the absence of the grass with its dense network of roots, the river would erode the banks of soft mud and meander back and forth from Kiawah Island to Johns Island on the other side; so that at one time the river might be far away and then again be under the doorsteps of homes on the marsh side of the island. There is a continual contest between the tight root mass for retention of the soil and the river sweeping it away. The plant roots are joined in this contest by the cooperative action of the ribbed mussels that fasten their shells to the roots by strong fibers called byssus. Thus the molluscs form a bulwark reminiscent of the riprap that man uses to stabilize banks.

The marsh has another important role; it serves as the nursery for huge numbers of marine organisms by providing food and shelter. Decaying grass contributes the vast bulk of the detritus that is the basic food, but other important contributions come from the algae that grow on the mud and the plankton brought in from the sea by each tide.

Added to this huge food supply is the large amount of animal and plant life also brought into the marsh on each tide. This life comes both from the freshwater streams inland and the salt water of the sea. The salinity of the river varies greatly from day to day, as these two sources of fresh and salt water mix;

heavy rains raise the amount of fresh water, storms at sea push more seawater into the river and render it more saline. Most of the animals and plants brought into the marsh by the tidal flow cannot adjust to these large changes in salinity and perish in the marsh; thus adding their bodies to the food supply.

The juvenile stages of most crabs, fish and shrimp also are carried into the marsh by the tidal flow. However, these organisms can withstand the fluctuations in salinity. The larger fishes that would consume these juvenile stages dare not penetrate the dense stand of spartina, and those that do often become entrapped and perish when the water recedes. Thus, abundant food and shelter make the marsh an ideal nursery; and, as the juveniles mature and leave the marsh for the open sea, their multitudes renew the oceans for another year.

But above and beyond all these benefits, the visual impact of that vast expanse is its most rewarding attribute for most of us. The Kiawah river in the distance is defined by the shimmer of open water and the sight of the occasional boat with its sails skimming over the marsh like the white wings of the egret. Closer, the islands in the marsh resemble ships in a sea of grass; all sailing the same east-west course for they are the remnants of the same ancient dunes that make up Kiawah itself. The view is rendered even more dramatic by the approach of a storm coming off Johns Island— an event so small and insignificant in the distance, so powerful when it suddenly sweeps over the marsh and hits with its full fury. In sunnier times, it is peaceful to watch the slow progress of cloud shadows and the wind patterns as the marsh grass bends in response. Add the majestic sweeping strokes of the Great Blue heron, the meandering course of a small family of raccoons heading out at low tide or the Lilliputian battles and courtships of the Fiddler crabs at our feet, and the scene is complete.

Nesting Reports

Bluebirds are checking out their boxes all over the island.

A pair of Ospreys was mating at one of the old nests on the first day of March—earlier than usual.

Eggs of the Great Horned owls have hatched in the nest along Ocean Course Drive. After my initial announcement in the winter, some of you may have mentally pictured the poor parent hunkered down in the nest to shelter eggs from cold winds and rain. You may have wondered why they chose such an inauspicious time. As for most birds, the nest time and place are determined by the time and place of maximum food availability. Those small eating-machines in the nest clamor all day or in the case of owls all night for food, more, more food. At only limited times of the year is the supply adequate to meet that demand. For the owl, rodents are the main food source, and those are most readily found before the new spring foliage obscures the ground.

(Bald eagles also nest in the winter, and with the increasing number of eagles seen on Kiawah, a nesting might occur here some year. For the eagle, the availability of fish for the nestlings is greatest in early spring because at that time pond water is clearest and the fish are sluggish from the cold.)

The Great Horned owls abruptly abandoned their nest shortly after the eggs hatched. Perhaps the chicks perished or were taken by a hawk, although it is difficult to imagine any predator audacious enough to try to slip by those ferocious owls. Now, a pair of Ospreys have been mating and refurbishing the nest, and perhaps their family will be more fortunate.

Turtle Nesting Started Early this Year.

In early March, the turtle patrol was requested to demonstrate our summertime activities for 32 visitors in connection with a Nature Symposium sponsored by the Town of Kiawah Island and Kiawah Island Resort. A team of six members of the patrol quickly assembled to do what we could to present a meaningful demonstration of the Loggerhead turtle nest protection that occurs on the island all summer long. Bill Connellee acted as the official greeter at the registration desk, but the other five of us were presented with a more difficult assignment; how could we demonstrate what we do on the beach in summer? The turtles were scattered throughout the ocean, with no thoughts yet of sex, and certainly not of nest building. So they were of no help. However, we did enact the summer scene as closely as possible. On the day before the demonstration, we were busy constructing nests as realistically as possible and practicing crawl marks in the sand.

The following morning was cold and windy on the beach; nevertheless, the patrol members were out in their flimsy turtle-shirts that are the standard dress of the summer—the visitors were more sensibly garbed in windbreakers and gloves. After a brief orientation to set the scene, the turtle patrol, consisting of Carl and Margit Obern arrived in the turtle patrol truck with lights flashing, looking for the marks of turtle nesting crawls. "Here is one now!", and indeed there was the crawl track for it had just been created the hour before by rake and trowel. Once the nest area was located, the patrol probed and "found" the nest. "Yes, it is a nest for here are the eggs just beneath the sand!" (My, they look just like ping-pong balls.) These eggs (or were they ping-pong balls?) were carefully removed and relocated in a more secure location toward the dunes. The new nest was protected by wire screening in case a raccoon or fox had a secret craving for ping-pong balls, sorry, turtle eggs.

Then, the story of the two-months-long incubation period was carried along at another planted nest that displayed the exit tracks from a hatching nest and still a third nest with hatched eggs that looked amazingly like crushed ping-pong balls to demonstrate that hatching had occurred. Now, it was time to tally up the results and determine hatching success. George Walther and Joan Wassen enacted that scene. Joan was outstanding and the actress up for the academy award as she gently probed the nest and joyfully liberated a hatchling which she brought up from the nest cavity and carefully placed on the sand. Even we in the know expected the ceramic replica to scramble toward the water!

For a cool and breezy day in March, it was a very successful simulation of the real thing that will be repeated many times during the hot summer days. Then, we will wish for a return of the cool breeze that chilled us as we dug that first nest of the season.

Some Creatures That Come To Kiawah Are Among the Untouchables.

Far out in the blue waters of the Atlantic, uncountable millions of a strangely beautiful jellyfish bob up and down on the waves like small balloons of brilliant blue to pink or purple hues. A thin-walled sac, filled with nitrogen gas, acts as a sail; and the jellyfish, responding to the prevailing winds and the ocean current, follow the Gulf Stream as it flows north. At any season of the year, a storm with several days of on-shore winds will drive them off course; and a few of these strange organisms, sailing along with long purple tentacles streaming behind for as much as 50 feet, approach the Carolina coast. Swimmers, aware that they share the water with many creatures of the sea, should have no difficulty seeing the bobbing blue floats on top of the waves and keep a respectful distance.

Finally, the sea will cast them high on the beach, and we can identify them as the Portuguese Man-of- war. This famous wanderer probably acquired its name from it worldwide distribution and its formidable armament. On shore, no beachcomber could miss them, and there is a temptation to bend down and pick up such a beautiful and exotic creature. Don't, unless you are wearing rubber gloves, because the tentacles carry one of the most severe stings of any animal in the sea. Exercise extreme caution even with dried specimens, because tentacles retain their stinging power for a long time and even dried cells may revive when moistened.

These cells are called nematocysts. Each one has a triggerlike bristle projecting from the surface, and inside the nematocyst a long tube lies neatly coiled. When the trigger is disturbed, the tube suddenly flies out and becomes embedded in whatever caused the disturbance, a fish or a hand brushing too close— and the toxic dose is injected. Even exposure to a few of the stings can inflict severe burns and blisters, and I'm unaware of any effective first aid treatment except the customary application of alcohol—externally of course. The exact nature of the poison is unknown, but probably several toxins are involved that produce paralysis of the nervous system. This may lead to extreme prostration if a very large dose is received; therefore, drowning of a swimmer after being stung is the greatest danger.

The Man-of-war has only one known natural enemy, the sea turtle. Deep-sea fishermen relate sightings of turtles, in the midst of great pastures of the organisms, eagerly munching away on the tentacles. They seem to go into a feeding frenzy and madly gorge themselves despite the stinging cells. However, the turtles are not immune to the toxins, and their eyes become swollen and red. Afterward, they seem to lose coordination, and wallow slackly in the waves. While in this condition, they are much less responsive, and will not dive beneath the water at the approach of a boat the way turtles normally do. Perhaps it is then that they are most vulnerable to sharks and lose portions of their flippers which in turn accounts for their varied crawl patterns when they come ashore to nest.

One marine animal that is apparently immune to the toxin is the Portuguese Man-of-war mackerel, a tiny fish that lives its life with impunity among the tentacles. It seems to act as a lure for other fish, drawing them in to be destroyed by its host while receiving protection and food particles as compensation.

Attention Bluebird Lady.

This playful comment is directed at the Bluebird Lady and her marvelous troops that so enthusiastically place bluebird boxes all over the island. For a number of years they have refined the design of the nestbox with the hopes of coming up with the perfect box that will gladden the heart of every bluebird on the island. Perhaps that concern is unnecessary; perhaps the bird is not all that particular about home design and location. I say this because a pair of bluebirds passed by all the lovely boxes and selected an iron pipe of 3" diameter that forms the gate at Fiddler's Run exit to the beach. And there they raised their family this spring. Each morning, as the gate was swung open by the turtle patrol, out she flew and waited in a nearby shrub until the gate was closed. Concerned folks thought she had made a serious mistake, and a beautiful bluebird box of the latest design was placed on a nearby dune. Thereafter, the male rested on top of the box and sang but home was still in the iron pipe.

Survival Is in Perilous Balance for The Only Seabird That Nests on Kiawah.

When a seabird is mentioned, probably most think of a gull or tern and maybe are not even sure of the difference between the two. Well, terns are generally smaller, more graceful birds than the stocky gulls. With their trim shape and long pointed wings they seem the perfection of aerodynamic design. They are the ones that hover and then dive beneath the waves for the tiny fish that they flaunt in their beaks as they rise with a shake to free their feathers of water.

Terns, to the uninformed eye, are all very much the same, but an ornithologist distinguishes them by the color of their beaks. Least terns have yellow beaks, Common terns have red with a black tip, Sandwich tern beaks are black with yellow tips, etc. During courtship, these beaks are brandished before potential mates as conspicuously as possible - pointing them up, then down and then waving them about.

The Least tern, as the name implies, is the smallest of the terns; diminutive, elegant, immaculate in its white and black plumage. From time immemorial they have nested in large colonies on the open shale of barrier beaches—an extremely perilous location for such an undertaking. There has always been a delicate balance between surviving the natural disasters of storms, high tides and predators in sufficient numbers to maintain the population from generation to generation.

The natural predators in the past have included raccoons, ghost crabs and birds such as gulls and crows. Reinforced by their numbers in colonial nesting, they have usually been successful in keeping those predators at bay. Storms and tides have taken the greatest toll. Flooding of the low beach zones by exceptionally high tides sometimes can destroy all the nests in a colony. In a storm, sand can drift over eggs and chicks and so alter the landmarks that the parents cannot find them, or the rain may wash eggs from the nest and drown chicks. Then, the only recourse is to make a new nest, deposit more eggs and start over.

The dainty beauty of the Least tern was nearly its undoing when in the 1880s it became the fashion for ladies' hats to be adorned with bird plumes. The little tern was so lovely that naturally a lady just had to have a stuffed one in her Easter bonnet. The balance began to tip toward extinction and only a few colonies remained on isolated islands in the northeast by the time fashions changed and the slaughter was outlawed about 1920. (An engaging account of this period was given in the July, 1994 issue of the Smithsonian magazine.)

With protection, their numbers came back, and they were once abundant in the late 1930s and early 1940s, with the center of population in the Carolinas. Since then they have steadily declined with the building of bridges to once lonely beaches, real estate development, the human population explosion along the coast and the attendant increase in predators such as dogs, foxes, raccoons, and hogs. The nest, just a shallow scrape in the sand, the tiny tan and brown speckled eggs and the fluffy chicks about the size of marbles, are so perfectly camouflaged that people, dogs, horses and vehicles trample them without even being aware of their existence. Currently they are not on the federal endangered species list, but several state wildlife agencies, including South Carolina, classify them as a threat-ened species.

On Kiawah, two colonies of the Least tern are known to have nested since observations were first recorded in the Environ-mental Inventory survey made by the Kiawah Island Co. in 1974. One colony was at the west end toward Seabrook, and I promise to relate at another time how that colony was lured away to Seabrook. The second colony, in the center of the island and near the present location of the Beach Club, was much more exposed to harassment by humans, their pets and vehicles by the time I first took an interest in them in the early 1980s. The beach safari would pass close by numerous times daily during the nesting season, and most of the parents would rise in alarm just as they would for any other disturbance they deemed a potential danger to the colony. The flurry of tiny white birds whirling overhead added to the spirit of adventure for the safari guests, but did not enhance the success rate of the colony.

My records show that this colony was destroyed by a high tide in 1985. The following year the colony moved around the island to become established at the extreme eastern end along the Stono river. Perhaps the loss of nests the previous year combined with the increased traffic on the beach motivated the move. Whatever the reason, the new site was not an improvement, and I quote from a paper that I wrote regarding the colony:

"A large loss of eggs in the period June 3-10 resulted from a series of storms. Winds from the northeast leveled the low dunes and covered many nests. Then, exceptional spring tides produced water levels 2 feet above the normal high tide and the entire colony was flooded. At that point, the parents abandoned the site."

During the following two years they appeared as usual about the 1st of May but made no attempt to nest at the former site near the Beach Club nor at the alternate one around on the Stono. Once, they did display an interest in the beach-like expanse of the Ocean Golf Course as Pete Dye was in the process of its first rough grading, and they came down in a flock to inspect it. I well remember that I was with Pete at the time and casually remarked that they might start nesting there which would mean that they could not be disturbed for another month or so. Pete took a step back and I saw a paleness creep beneath his tan, but he said nothing. However, the next day all his heavy equipment was racing about and furiously moving sand back and forth. The terns got the message.

So, has the balance tilted once again toward extinction? No, don't underestimate these terns; they demonstrated a remarkable adaptability, and have found another site for their nesting colonies. Where could that be? I'll give you a clue; it's in the busy commercial and industrial zones of our cities. My answer will appear in a later story.

Unusual Bird Sighting.

I saw an immature Reddish egret foraging in a tidal trough on our beach on the morning of August 29th. This is an unusual species to see this far north, but the juveniles customarily wander afar. The immature bird is slightly smaller than our Common Egret, mostly a uniform brownish gray color and with black legs and bill. The last time I saw the species here was in 1986 when three immature birds lingered at Ibis pond for a week in July. It is always nice to be surprised by these unexpected visitors.

Sea Turtles Are Having A Banner Season.

Loggerhead turtles have nested in exceptional numbers during the first half of this season. On June 30th we had our 126th nest, to be compared with 96 nests for the entire 1993 season. At the close, we may have a record- breaker of well over 200 nests. The volunteers often put in a full morning of work before some of us are up, and occasionally in weather that makes the beach a lonely place, but they seem to be thriving on it! Several have had the thrill of seeing the female still at the nest.

Probably the most exciting encounter was with an exceptionally large turtle that become lost on the stormy night of June 27th and ended up wandering about on the practice green of the Ocean Course. Greenskeeper George Frye and three of his crew loaded her in the back of my pickup truck. That was no easy task for she must have weighed over 300 lbs and was so strong that she could brush a man aside with a wave of a flipper. Once in the truck, she was quite docile and allowed herself to be unloaded on the beach without a struggle; perhaps the sight and sound of the surf soothed her, and after resting several minutes she departed. Really, she should have been quite familiar with our beach, because her crawl pattern indicated that she had already nested here on May 29th and June 16th.

Many people on the beach after dark also have seen turtles coming and going from nests, and most have been careful to extinguish flashlights and keep a good distance from the animal so that it is not frightened. Also, most property owners along the beach have done well to extinguish outside lighting on the ocean side, and renters have been very cooperative when informed of the purpose for the slogan, "Lights Out For Turtles." The Great Mother Turtle who dwells at the bottom of the sea thanks you, and I thank you too.

Returning along the beach late one night after inspection for lighting, I noticed the long black line of a turtle crawl etched on the moonlit beach and pointing to her dark mass vaguely discernible in the front dune. Quietly approaching, I saw that egg laying was complete; she was in the act of covering and concealing the nest. All four flippers were flailing and sand was flying everywhere as she turned this way and that to make it as difficult as possible for the fox and the turtle patrol to find that nest. Departing, she made the 100 yard dash to the water's edge in 17 minutes—pretty good time for a turtle.

As I watched her leave, with the black silhouette of our island behind me, a three-quarter moon high overhead and the turtle disappearing in the breaking surf, I felt transported back to the Mesozoic era—an obvious impossibility because *Homo sapiens* has traveled little more than a million years down that incredible passage of time, and Kiawah Island had yet to be built from sands yet to be brought down from mountains yet to be formed. But there were other beaches and early ancestors of this turtle were there, performing the same ritual, beneath the same moon for those millions and millions of years. Perhaps awareness of that awesome history accounts for the hard work so many volunteers do to ensure that the turtles continue. Mother T. and I thank you too!

Ospreys Are Having A Tough Season.

We often think of ospreys as having it easy. All they have to do is sail around, catch a fish now and then, and go home to the family secure in a nest high in the top of a tree. That is not always true as the following events will show.

The first was related by Joan Wassen who witnessed a classic predatory act that many of us have read about but few have been fortunate enough to actually witness. But let Joan tell it in her own words:

"While on the beach the afternoon of May 14th, I heard the cry of an osprey over land behind me. With my binoculars I saw the osprey with a fish in its talons, being chased by a mature Bald eagle. Just as they flew out over the ocean, not very high above the water, the eagle dive-bombed the osprey, who in turn released the fish. The eagle dropped down and caught the falling fish in mid-air. Then they both turned back toward land—each going its own way. This all happened so quickly I would have thought it a dream if my daughter and son-in-law were not there also to observe this special occasion."

The other events demonstrate that those high nests are not as secure as they seem. This spring we had two pairs of osprey nesting on Kiawah. Both nests were in undeveloped portions of the island in the vicinity of Willet pond. One was about 1 mile to the northeast and the other was about 1/2 mile to the south of that pond. Both nests had females incubating eggs in May. Just after eggs in the first nest hatched and parents were starting to feed the chicks, the nest was abruptly abandoned; and the parents did not return.

The second nest was more successful and by mid-June three chicks, about two-thirds the adult size, were hopping about and starting wing exercises. The next day all three chicks were missing and one parent was standing on the edge and occasionally peering down into the vacant nest as though wondering what had happened. What did happen? Because all three

chicks seemed healthy the previous day, loss to a predator seemed most probable. The experts tell us that young ospreys in the United States are prey to raccoons and Great Horned owls. Viewing the nests, both in the tops of tall pine trees that were dead and free of most branches, it seems like a difficult and dangerous climb even for the agile raccoon. My money would be on the horned owl, of which we have a number of pairs and indeed one pair successfully raised a family in the same nest where the three osprey chicks vanished so mysteriously. Is the horned owl so formidable that it can take such large, scrappy chicks? Again, the experts say yes, indeed there are records of horned owls catching adult ospreys on the nest at night and killing them. No wonder those ospreys are always looking over their shoulders.

The Leatherback

Occasionally the sea will bring to our shore the carcass of a monstrous reptile, and you, seeing it there in the surf, might think it had underdone a time warp and come from a steamy inland sea that it shared with the dinosaurs and other ancient reptiles. You would be correct, for its ancestors can be traced back to those prehistoric times. This relic is the most massive of all living reptiles. It has a 5 to 7 foot, tear-shaped body from which a relatively small head and four huge flippers protrude, and the entire beast is covered with a black, leathery hide. It is *Dermochelys coriacea*, "the turtle covered in leathery skin," the Leatherback. It is set apart from the other marine turtles not only by it size and leathery skin but also by the wide range of occurrence. All marine turtles occur in tropic and semi-tropic waters but only the Leatherback ventures into the cold northern and southern oceans, and there are even reports of sightings of Leatherbacks swimming among the icebergs. Its nesting habits are more conventional, and for that purpose it uses beaches in the tropical zone.

I had the opportunity several years ago to visit a Leatherback nesting beach on St Croix in the Virgin Islands. Unfortunately it was late in the nesting season and I did not see one of the massive black adults come out of the sea, illuminated only by the moon or starlight—this must be a sight to send a shiver of fright over the bravest. But I did participate in digging a nest at hatching time; as I held one of the 3 inch hatchlings in the palm of my hand it appeared to be an exact replica of the adult. I marveled that it would grow to a size equal to 10 times my own weight, and I am not aware of any other species of large animal that can duplicate that change of size.

For many years the general behavior of the animal remained a mystery; about all that was known was that the species occurred all over the world, that it seldom came into coastal waters except to nest, and it seemed to roam widely in its ceaseless pursue of jellyfish. More recently, tagging procedures, especially with electronic measuring and signaling devices have revealed many fascinating details about its capability and habits. For example, in 1970 a female was tagged on a nesting beach in Surinam before leaving the coast of South America. It must have crossed the Atlantic for it was found crawling ashore less than a year later in Ghana, West Africa. Not only did the distance of at least 3,700 miles set a new world's record but it also demonstrated for the first time that marine turtles do travel from one continent to another.

The prowess of this turtle and the structural and physiological adaptations that are being revealed by these modern studies probably contributed in large measure to its durability down all these millions of years. That this species, now classified as endangered, can continue to survive over the brief span of a few centuries that it has shared with modern man appears dubious.

Leave the First Aid to the Professionals When A Whale Comes to Kiawah.

Last winter I reported that a Short-finned pilot whale washed ashore dead in February; then, in the late afternoon of August 25th another whale, this one still alive, was observed in the surf between Beachwalker Park and the western tip of the island. A call came out from Security to George Walther and me as participants in the marine stranding network for the SC Department of Natural Resources. When we arrived in the town truck, the whale was struggling in the surf and seemed intent on beaching itself despite the efforts of three young people to push it back to sea. Our first action was to call the three back to shore. What they were doing was very dangerous. Even though small by whale standards, the 10.5 ft. animal weighed probably 800 lbs and could seriously injure a person either with a blow from its tail or by rolling over the person. Also, the whale was bleeding from multiple abrasions as it thrashed about on shell and sand, and the commotion and blood often will attract sharks. One of these could strike an arm or leg in the turbid water. Therefore, always heed this caution:

Caution #1: Never enter the water to help a stranded dolphin or whale.

From the truck I telephoned Sally Murphy, head of the marine stranding network for the state, and her advice was to leave the animal alone until she and her husband Tom could arrive from their home at Green Pond. While waiting, I noted that this whale did not have the sleek predatory cast of the pilot whale; instead, it had the massive shape that we associate with whales. Its head was squarish like the Sperm whale, and its underslung jaw was reminiscent of the shark. I learned that this species of Pygmy sperm whale, as it was later identified, is pelagic and ranges over most oceans of the world. Singly or in small groups, it feeds on Cephalopods (squid and octopus) as well as crabs and fish.

For the next hour George stayed with the still struggling animal until the Murphys arrived. They judged it near death on the basis of its behavior and extremely emaciated condition (ribs were clearly visible and even the bones of the flippers were discernible through the skin). With the aid of George and several observers that included Tom Fromme and his son Michael, the Murphys were able to slide a huge canvas stretcher beneath the whale and bring it to shore. Then, they winched it into the bed of their truck, and off they went to the laboratory at Fort Johnson with the flukes hanging out over the tailgate. At the lab, veterinarian Dr. Jean McKee, who tends to so many of our sick and injured birds, examined it and confirmed that it was near death—not too surprising considering the last few hours of its life! She euthanized it by an injection into the heart.

The next day a team of four from the laboratory, some of whom had been on our beach with the other whale, devoted a full day out on the lawn performing a very complete necropsy. (The report I received ran to six pages!) It related that the whale, a mature male, had three cookie-cutter scars from shark bites, a heavy load of internal parasites, and in addition to being badly malnourished was suffering from anemia and renal failure.

The multiple health problems of this unfortunate creature emphasizes a further precaution in approaching these animals. Most often when a whale or dolphin strands on our beach it is ill or seriously injured. As a mammal, its diseases may be transmissible to humans. This incident is a good example, because Tom Fromme had been in contact with the whale while helping to position it in the stretcher; within 24 hours he had an extensive rash on the arms and legs that necessitated treatment by his physician. Therefore, we have:

Caution #2: never come in contact with a stranded marine mammal unless wearing protective clothing and gloves.

so admire these creatures of the deep sea in their natural habitat, but let trained personnel of the wildlife department deal with the sick ones that wash ashore and may be afflicted with everything except ingrown toenails. And come to think of it, I guess they do have ingrown toenails.

The Not-So-Wild Wildlife
That Once Roamed Kiawah.

After the last share-cropper fields went fallow around 1919, Arnoldus Vanderhorst V continued until his death in 1943 to lease portions of Kiawah as pasturage for horses and cattle and the "running" of hogs. When C.C. Royal purchased the island in 1950, he continued to lease land, which by now had been largely overgrown with brush and trees, for pasturage of livestock. Tom Welch, caretaker of the island for Mr. Royal, and his partner from Summerville kept horses in fenced pastures, and a Mr. Kayze from Walterboro was allowed to run cattle and hogs at the eastern end. These were fenced off from the homes that were by now appearing along what would become Eugenia Avenue.

Later, Mr. Kayze removed the cattle, but the hogs remained free to roam. Tom Welch relates that he would occasionally shoot a hog for the meat, but probably their numbers were increasing. At the time the Kiawah Island Co. acquired control of the island in 1974, the hogs were destroying vegetation in the dunes by their rooting, and a man with a pack of dogs was hired to round up and remove them. (Unfortunately, the story of that roundup has been lost, but it must have been a heroic effort given the number of decades the hogs had run wild over the great expanse of marsh, swamp and forest.)

A small herd of horses, that included some saddle horses and others that had never been broken, remained on the island. Occasionally they would escape the fenced pasture, and I still vividly remember biking down one of the dirt roads in 1979 in the south pasture across Kiawah Island Parkway from what is now Night Heron Park. Suddenly I rounded a curve to arrive in the midst of the grazing herd. I don't know whether the herd or I was the more startled as I braked to a stop and they trotted down the road to stand as a compact mass with the colts peering cautiously around the flanks of the adults. Perceiving that I was harmless, they drifted back up the road and disappeared through an opening in the trees. Of course this delightful kind of encounter could not continue on the island because of the danger of collisions with automobiles and the potential for damage to the greens of the first golf course, Marsh Point. Tom Welch told me that shortly after my encounter the horses were taken off and sold at auction; another version is that they were shipped to a Walterboro slaughterhouse (*News and Courier*, October 30, 1979). Whatever the correct version, the horses are gone and now even the dirt road I passed over on the bike is rapidly being incorporated into the River golf course.

One other species on the island at that earlier time was a herd of goats. No one seems to know how they arrived on the island; the Royal children had a pet goat named Cindy but that is another story. According to Tom Welch the goat herd roamed the eastern end of the island, and some were shot by poachers who came ashore from time to time. What ultimately became of them remains behind the veil of time—could their descendants have grown long tails and become the mystical cougars so often reported?

The Brown Pelicans Had A Successful Nesting Season.

If you are one of the many compulsive counters of pelicans that fly over our island in seemingly endless processions, perhaps you have noted the numbers going up. The increase is due to the new crop of juveniles that have now fledged and joined the adults in the formation. It was quite an addition this year for the nesting season was good. Charlotte Hope of the S.C. Dept. of Natural Resources (formerly the Wildlife & Marine Resources Dept.) has informed me there were 4474 nests at 6 colonies in the state, and 2313 of those nests were on Bird Key

in the Stono river. The juveniles are distinguishable from the adults by the head plumage; heads of juveniles are covered with brown feathers, whereas feathers of the head and neck of an adult are white. The juveniles join with the adults in the formations as they learn the fine arts of locating and catching fish. This is a life or death training that juveniles must quickly master, otherwise they become too weak to fly and starvation is certain. If you encounter a weakened pelican on the beach, inform Security promptly for it may be saved. But leave the rescue to experienced people; otherwise the rescue effort can be so exhausting for the bird that it may die on the spot.

Fall Color in the Dune Fields.

The dunes are never a riot of color for bare survival is about all most of the plants can muster, but in the fall months some lovely colors are on display. It will not be gaudy, for the plants that live in that harsh environment are very modest. However, if you look carefully from almost any of the dune walkways, you will be treated to a warm autumn display.

As you walk down the boardwalk you are likely first to encounter one of the loveliest of the fall plants, the Mullenbergia or sweetgrass, as the basket-makers of the Charleston area call it, for the dried grass is the main component of their baskets. It is especially brilliant if backlighted by a lowering sun, for then the plumes are a rich red. If you arrive in the early morning, you may be in for a special treat because the dew-laden plumes assume a ghostly lavender cast.

Further down the boardwalk you will note the various shades of yellow contributed by Seaside goldenrod and Camphor weed, blue of Butterfly-pea and purple of the appropriately named Autumn bells. Further out on the front dunes these plants are displaced by the delicate pinks of Russian thistle, white of Fiddle-leaf morning-glory, browns and yellows of Seashore elder, and if you are on the right boardwalk the yellows and oranges of Evening primrose.

If you venture down to the western end of the island you will be greeted by large expanses of dark red from Glasswort and Sea purslane that seem to grow well only on the saltflats at that locale. So get out on these brisk fall days, breath deeply of the clean air, feel the salt spray on your cheeks and watch for those magical spots of color in the dunes.

The Plight of A Duck Out of Water.

About a week before Thanksgiving, golfers coming off the Osprey course excitedly informed me that I must see the flock of mallards that were protectively huddled around a cripple near the fifth tee. When I arrived in mid-afternoon, the flock of three drakes and ten hens were huddled together so compactly that it would have been impossible to slide a card between any two of them. When a golf cart passed close by, they arose in alarm, and I could see that two of the hens were crippled. Had the flock been protecting them? Not so, for when they settled again in a tight cluster the two cripples were left on the periphery. The lagoon beside the fairway may have attracted the flock initially, but it did not look as inviting after I counted eleven 3 to 4 foot alligators either in the water or along the bank. I was puzzled, the mallards did not act like wild birds, were they the tame flock that usually paddle about on Sparrow pond by the Inn?

Inquiry quickly provided the answer. The Wildlife & Fisheries Committee had purchased 100 pen-raised mallards one week previously and released them—60 at the west end and 40 at the east end of the island. I could now understand the behavior of the birds, all tightly clustered together. Poor ducks, they were totally unprepared for the dangers of life on Kiawah. They didn't know an alligator from a bobcat, to say nothing of the foxes and raccoons that patrol the fairways and pond edges nightly.

It was easy to follow the misfortunes of the ducks, because they remained at the 5th hole as though uncertain where else to go. Three days after my first visit, the two cripples and two of the drakes were missing. Another three days, and only one drake and three hens were left. Finally, at dusk, the drake and two remaining hens waddled forlornly along the lagoon edge; if I could have gathered them up, I would have taken them home. Next morning, the drake and one hen were sound asleep on the fairway at 9 o'clock of a sunny day, what a rough night! The next morning both were gone, and golfers reported none were to be seen on the course.

In hindsight, the money and effort might have been better spent on restoration of one or two of the larger ponds to attract once again the migratory ducks that came here each winter by the hundreds a decade ago.

WINTER, 1994

Wood Storks Are Nesting in Charleston County For the First Time

The Wood stork is an infrequent visitor to Kiawah, but when present it makes a dramatic addition to our ponds. The bird, sometimes referred to as the Wood ibis, has the distinction of being the only species of stork in North America. It once occurred in all the coastal states between Texas and South Carolina, but the greatest numbers were in Florida. Recently however, the population in Florida has declined sharply. Much of this decline can be attributed to human manipulation of the water table throughout the Everglades. Unfortunately, storks are very selective in nest location and prefer to place nests high in cypress trees surrounded by water so that there is protection from predators. Consequently, the stork has been placed on the endangered species list, and the birds have ranged increasingly northward into Georgia and South Carolina in search of suitable nesting habitat.

Mark Dodd, a young biologist in the S.C. Department of Natural Resources, tells me that there were 712 Wood stork nests in the state this year in seven colonies. Last year, there were 806 nests in three colonies. These numbers do not demonstrate trends because the storks do not nest separately but join egrets and herons in various established colonies. Also, nesting depends upon rainfall, and storks will not even build nests when conditions are unlikely to provide sufficient food for the chicks.

This year they nested in Charleston County for the first time at a rookery near Ravenel. By mid-summer, the young had fledged and the storks had left that secluded site. From late summer into early winter, they fly over lowcountry wetlands in search of food and this is our best opportunity for viewing them. Soaring high overhead, these huge birds on wings that span 5 ½ feet are magnificent. A striking black and white wing pattern and extended neck and legs form the shape of a large cross. They seek ponds in which the water level is down so that fish are concentrated in shallow pools, and are attracted there by the sight of egrets and herons already feeding. Then, down they come to join in the feast.

Their feeding style is amusing to watch. With an ungainly gait that is accentuated by their 3 ft. height, they meander slowly through the shallows with heads down. The long beaks are held partially open and swung slowly through the water. Those bills that look so hard and lifeless actually must be exquisitely sensitive. When the bill contacts a fish it snaps shut instantly. Often they feed in groups as each bird shuffles through the shallow water and stirs up the bottom with its feet to flush concealed fish into the open. Then it is a very lucky fish that evades all those snapping bills. They are so successful in this maneuver that you often will see them followed by one or more egrets and herons that hope to be first at apprehending the fleeing fish.

Later, they may roost in the trees near the pond edge. So watch for them at such times. You will easily distinguish them from the white egrets by their greater size and dark, featherless heads.

The Very Essence of A Barrier Island Is Change

Those who drive along Kiawah Island Parkway and Govenors Drive cannot help but be aware that big changes are underway. On all sides they view the huge machines removing trees, digging ponds and creating hills as the River Course is shaped. Some deplore this alteration—and it certainly is drastic—but perhaps they could place these changes in some perspective if they realized that barrier islands are in continual change. These islands of sand are formed during cycles of changing sea level and are continually modified thereafter to meet other changing conditions.

Modern radioactive dating of clam shells at various depths in the foundations of Kiawah indicate that it formed some 3000-

4000 years ago. In that period of rising sea level, sand accumulated at the roots of a more ancient landmass estimated to date back about 50,000 years. Those roots are located beneath what we call Rhetts Bluff and along a portion of the Kiawah Island Parkway. Even now the Carolina coast imperceptibly is migrating in response to the rising sea level. (An article in the Post and Courier on November 1, 1994 told of the recent discovery by divers of the remains of a cypress forest that dates back just 10,000 years; today, remnants of that forest are 15 miles off shore!) Peat beds that show up through the beach sand at the eastern end of Kiawah tell the same story. They formed in the marsh behind the island and it is possible to find embedded in them the shells of oysters and species of clams that grow only in the marsh. Since the time the shells were embedded, the island has migrated shoreward until those ancient beds now reappear on the seaward side of the island.

Once the sandbar that was destined to become Kiawah Island had grown to a sufficient size to have some stability, vegetation became established. It probably then resembled other undisturbed barrier islands that exist today, clothed in brush and a mixture of palmettos, pines and hardwoods. But once established, Kiawah did not remain undisturbed. Because it is built of sand, the island responded to storms and ocean currents that continually alter the size and shape of its perimeter, and I will discuss this in a later section concerning the beach. In the interior, the vegetation was destroyed many times by hurricanes and by fires arising from lightning or set by Indians.

When the Europeans arrived other changes occurred. For the first time the island was 'owned,' and the owners viewed it as a resource to be used for their profit. Indications are that early in the 18th Century it was used as a cattle range; the animals were conveniently confined to the island and there was a plentiful supply of salt hay (*Spartina patens*) along the marsh as excellent fodder. With the realization of the value of the land for the raising of indigo and later cotton (it was not suitable for rice, the third cash crop of the coastal Carolinas), the island underwent an additional large change. A map dated 1854 shows that contiguous fields occupied the entire middle third of the island, and the 1860 tax records list 800 acres of improved and 1700 acres of unimproved land as well as over 100 slaves among other household possessions. (For your comparison, a century and a half later the River Course will encompass a little over 300 acres of the same 'improved' land.)

Following the Civil War and the general stagnation of the southern economy, the fields were abandoned and nature began to reclothe the island in brush and trees. By the time of the purchase of the island by C. C. Royal in 1950 that transition was well along. Under the ownership of Mr. Royal a different set of changes began. He viewed the island from a lumberman's perspective and extensively removed marketable pine. One exception was at the eastern end where Coastguardsmen at the time of the First World War had put so many steel-jacketed bullets in the trees that saw blades were destroyed at his mills. It was at this time that most of the large ponds on the island were created by diking off fingers of the marsh. Also, the old logging roads became the forerunners of our Kiawah Island Parkway, Govenors Drive and Ocean Course Drive.

With the purchase of the island in 1974 by Kiawah Island Co., a different cast of owners took central stage. They set in motion a different series of changes that continue to this day. Perhaps some of the recent changes are good and some are bad—certainly the visit by hurricane Hugo in 1989 was bad by any standard. A decision on the merits of these changes will vary with the viewer, but changes will continue for that is the very essence of barrier islands.

Distemper Is Sweeping Through the Fox and Raccoon Populations on the Island.

Kiawah Island Security began receiving reports of sick foxes toward the end of November. The first of these was diagnosed as having canine distemper. As the fatalities increased, it quickly became evident that this was the beginning of an epidemic which first spread through the fox and then the raccoon populations. A similar epidemic had begun two months earlier on Seabrook Island and probably was the source of the infection here. This is a respiratory disease, and the virus, Paramyxovirus by name, is highly infectious for dogs as well as the foxes and raccoons, because it is easily transmitted from one animal to another simply by close contact and inhalation of the viral particles. The town office promptly issued a warning that was distributed at the main security gate, and to date no reports have been received of the infection in pet dogs.

From the first day onward, Security personnel under the direction of Major Seabrook have been busy bringing in dead or dying foxes and raccoons. The infected animals are noosed, placed in cages for transportation to security headquarters and immediately euthanized to end their suffering. Chief of Security Bill Westberg has been concerned about the possibility of rabies creeping in and passing undetected amongst the sick animals that his personnel must collect. However, rabid animals are aggressive and high strung whereas these animals stricken with the distemper are lethargic and disoriented. Personnel have been well trained by Major Seabrook and take all precautions not to handle the animals directly, and if behavior of the animal suggests even the possibility of rabies, tests will be made immediately.

By the end of December, 23 foxes and 16 raccoons had been picked up. In the past two weeks only 9 of the foxes but all 16 of the raccoons were infected. Therefore, it would appear that the epidemic is subsiding amongst the foxes and just now raging amongst the raccoons. Many more of both species lie uncounted in the woods, dunes and marsh, so that the populations of both species have been truly decimated.

Jean Pfaff of the Sea Island Veterinarian Clinic informs me that viral diseases such as this occur cyclically in wild animal populations as numbers build up and normal territorial separation is no longer possible. As the epidemic subsides, the survivors possess an immunity to the disease which lasts for three or four years; by then, crowding occurs once again and the cycle repeats itself—it is simply nature's way of self regulation.

Bird Sightings

Shortly after the New year, as I was doing my periodic inspection of Ocean Course ponds for ducks and other waterfowl, I was delighted to see five Snow geese on the pond at the 16th hole. These beautiful Arctic geese seldom are seen this far south but watch for them later this winter. They are the only geese you are likely to see on the southeast coast with heads and necks all in white. They come in two color morphs, white and blue; the ones I saw were of the blue phase—once thought to be a separate species and called the "blue goose."

On my way home, my day was really made by spotting an adult Bald eagle on the old osprey nest across Bass creek at Willet pond. While I watched, it walked in and out of the nest cavity and really gave it a critical inspection as would any prospective homeowner. The nest seemed ridiculously small for the huge bird but such nest usurpations do occur.

Another Successful Nesting of Loggerhead Turtles in 1994.

The season started early. On a raw March morning, some of our most dedicated volunteers were out on the beach to demonstrate for attendees of the Nature Symposium how we protect turtle nests in the summer (as reported in the spring). Then, nesting actually began on May 10th. Prior to the 1993 nesting season, the beach had been badly eroded into steep banks very much like the ones formed again this winter. Happily the beach had been restored by 1994 to a normal gentle contour by the action of winter winds and waves. Therefore, it was possible to leave most nests near their original sites, and thus retain a natural distribution over the total beach area. It was fortunate that we were able to do so and not resort to the more labor intensive relocation of nests into zones as in 1993, because the season turned out to be one of high numbers of nests, both at Kiawah and all along the Carolina coast.

Our volunteers numbered 99—an increase of 12 over the previous year. This included 21 with five years or more of experience on the program. Those on the nesting patrols located and protected 197 nests. In addition, 7 nests were totally destroyed before the arrival of the patrol, and 11 "wild" nests were found by the hatching patrols at the time of hatching. Therefore, a total of 215 nests were made on the beach in 1994. This was considerably higher than the average of 154 nests/year for 1972-92 and approaches the highest recorded number of 225 in 1990.

Foxes totally destroyed 7 nests and partially destroyed 30% of the marked nests prior to arrival of the patrol. This represents a serious loss. Baited tracking stations revealed a rather uniform distribution of foxes along the beach with about the same numbers in May and in July. This suggested that the summer nesting did not attract them to the beach. Instead, foxes at the east end, where predation was heaviest, apparently were more aware of the nests and more knowledgeable about digging into them. Probably this expertise is passed along from generation to generation, because we frequently observed the tracks of both adult and juvenile foxes following right up the crawl made by the turtle as she sought a nesting site. When we arrived in the morning, all that remained was the open, raided nest. The only effective protection would be patrols through-out each night. Any volunteers?

Other teams covered the entire eight mile nesting area each day by foot and bike patrols as the time for hatching ap-proached. They were able to personally escort 2094 of the sturdy little hatchlings to the ocean—probably the most mean-ingful measure of success of the program for them. In addition, they kept accurate records on the progress of the hatching and the numbers of eggs successfully hatched in each nest. The average hatching success rate was 70%. This high success rate, in a year with 66% of the nests relocated, speaks well for the skill of our volunteers in the relocation procedure and for the protective program in general.

Mother turtles added zest to the season, as they often will. One nesting female became lost in a storm and ended up on the Ocean Course the next morning, as I related last summer. An-other did not complete her nest in front of Shipwatch until 8:30 AM; by then a lane had to be formed through the crowd of spectators to permit her to find the ocean and depart. The photography shop did a great business that day!

Postscript: I inspected the beach on Oct 14 following the very heavy rains in the first part of the month. The standing water in the dunes and the beach wet even at low tide with the ground water draining out beneath the sand, once again made me realize how sensitive the nesting season is to the weather. Had those rains occurred in July, every nest would have been flooded with loss of the entire season.

Those White-headed Ducks on Our Ponds This Winter

We are fortunate this winter to have some fascinating migra-tory ducks on many of our ponds. These are the Hooded mergansers which I hereafter will refer to as 'Hoodies,' a name that is affectionately given to them. A small flock of about a dozen arrive each fall at about Thanksgiving and spend the winter on Willet pond. This year a much larger number of Hoodies chose Kiawah ponds for their winter vacation from the cold north. They are less sociable than most other diving ducks, and you will usually see them in small parties of 15 or less.

When you see ducks on a pond, look at the heads, for the male Hoodies signal their identity by a pronounced white patch on the side of the head—the females are more modestly covered in brown. As a minor complication in your sorting of these migrants, we have a second species of diving ducks that also have some white on the head. These are the Bufflehead sea ducks that spend the winter in large flocks called rafts floating offshore; occasionally some come in to some of the larger ponds near the ocean. I have see them on Ibis and Willet ponds as well as the large pond near the 16th hole of the Ocean Course. They are smaller than the Hoodies and with much more white on the body so are easily distinguished.

Returning to the Hoodies, these engaging little diving ducks have a bushy crest at the rear of the head and a slender bill with teeth-like structures for catching and holding small fish, thereby earning another nickname of "sawbill." As briefly mentioned, the male is distinctive with a bushy black head and white blaze behind the eye that may be visible as either a rectangular patch or a massive white area depending on whether the crest is closed or elevated. They begin to choose mates in mid-winter; therefore, there is a great amount of courtship of the females and rivalry between males occurring on our ponds. It is amusing to observe them elevate and lower the white hoods as males signal rival males in communications beyond our understanding and dash about in pursuit of one another. The male gives every sign of strutting before the hens—is it possible for a duck to strut in the water? In any event he shows himself in the best possible light in hopes the lovely female will choose him as her mate before they all leave in May for the breeding grounds in our northern states and Canada. There, they nest in tree cavities in wooded areas near rivers and small lakes—much the same terrain they have chosen on Kiawah for the winter.

Other Black and White Ducks Off Our Beach

Toward the end of January it was possible to observe from anywhere on the Kiawah beach large numbers of birds on the ocean. With the unaided eye, they appeared as black dots about a quarter of a mile out from shore. With the aid of a spotting scope they could be identified as Scaup and numbered in the thousands. Associated with some of the flocks were a few Red- throated loons and Red-breasted mergansers; usually these appeared as single birds or pairs. The Scaup feed in the ocean on small crustaceans and molluscs in the winter, and they spend their summers in large freshwater ponds up north. Therefore, it is not too surprising to find some of the Scaup on Kiawah ponds; in fact, there are eight of them on the segment of Canvasback pond in back of our home as I write this article. Watch for them; they are the small dark ducks with white side panels.

Excellent Sites for Viewing the Marsh

In an earlier story I extolled the values of the marsh and the enjoyment of viewing it. And yet, the viewing is sometimes difficult if you are not fortunate enough to have a home along the marsh. Therefore, I would like to bring to your attention two good viewing sites that might not occur to you. These are our viewing towers. One is in Marsh Island Park that extends into the marsh roughly in the middle of Kiawah. Unfortunately, parking is still not available but the bike path along Govenors Drive goes right by it. The park was established in 1980 and I can still remember my surprise and joy to be biking down the dirt clearing that was destined to become Govenors Drive and suddenly encountering an asphalt path to Marsh Island. As I passed over the new boardwalk to the island I thought to myself, "This is my kind of developer; his priorities match mine!" As soon as I returned home I wrote a note of appreciation to Saleh Alzouman, president of Kiawah Island Co. And I received a prompt reply!

If you take that same path, you will get your first view of the marsh at low level from that boardwalk. Then continue to the tower to view the scene from a higher elevation. The tower, damaged by hurricane Hugo, has been restored and is available to all that can manage one or two flights of stairs. From the top you will be rewarded with a magnificent view of the marsh, the Kiawah river and Johns Island beyond. It is beautiful at any time but to watch storm clouds as they menacingly roll over from Johns Island is a special treat; but hasten down as they cross the river or you will be forced to wait out the storm on the tower!

I am sure that the second tower is less well known but it provides an even more spectacular view. It is the centerpiece of Marsh View Tower park at the western end of Kiawah. To reach it, drive down to the end of Marsh Hawk Lane, where there is ample parking. The tiny park was the first to be established on Kiawah in 1977-78. The twenty-five foot tower also was rebuilt after Hugo. It has a tight iron spiral of 36 steps with a platform half-way up, and the ascent is perfectly safe—even for an oldie moldie with a fear of heights such as myself.

The view is well worth the climb, for it provides a panoramic sweep that ties Kiawah and Johns Islands together via the connector bridge as well as showing the immensity of the marsh that carpets all the intervening space. Views are spectacular at any time but my preference is high tide, for then creeks are full and you will readily appreciate that you are on an island separated from the mainland by a watery domain.

Update on the Canine Distemper Epidemic.

On February 21st I checked on the state of the epidemic with Major Seabrook of Security. He informed me that no animals had been brought in during the past week and that the tally stood at 55 raccoons and 43 Gray foxes. (Red foxes have been seen on the island in the past few years, but none have been found among the casualties so far.) The figures on January 6th as I reported earlier were 36 foxes and 26 raccoons; therefore, it would appear that the epidemic is now subsiding. As I mentioned before, these numbers do not include the many animals that lie uncounted in the woods, dunes and marsh. Truly this has been a serious loss. How serious is a question we should address soon.

Bluebirds Need Volunteers

The Bluebird Box Program is now being supported by the new Wildlife Committee of the town, but efforts of volunteers are the heart and soul of the program. Now, the bluebirds are returning and in need of new nest boxes and renovation of existing ones. Joan Smith tells me that volunteers are needed immediately to inspect, repair and install boxes. In April through June volunteers will be needed to monitor boxes on a weekly basis. Sign up now and learn how you can support the nesting of these beautiful birds. Call Glen or Joan Smith.

Great Horned Owl Nesting.

In February I observed a pair of Great Horned owls nesting again this year (and they do not need any volunteer help, thank you!) The site this year is the old Osprey nest across Bass creek from Willet Pond. With a spotting scope, I could make out the head of the sitting female, and especially as she turned her head to scan for intruders, I could see the two tufts of feathers jutting up like ears. She is on eggs at this time for, as you know by now, their nesting season comes early in the year.

By April, the owls had hatchlings in the nest. I became aware of this when I noted the female sitting considerably higher in the nest after 30 days. That is right on target for the reported average incubation time. I was certain of the hatching on the next day. Viewing the nest through the spotting scope, I made out a large dark object blowing up and down in the wind, but I could not identify it. It looked like a wing but surely the owl was not sharing her nest with another bird! Then the owl began to feed the newly hatched young and the black object was no longer to be seen. I must conclude that she had caught a large black bird—probably a crow—and brought it back to the nest. If you locate the nest and see that the parent is not there, be patient and watch carefully. She is almost certain to return soon and if she glides in on wings spanning 4½ feet and with a rodent gripped in one talon, your wait will be well rewarded.

Activity at the owl nest is not the only excitement there at this time, because a pair of Ospreys have set up housekeeping in a second old nest. The two nests are high in the tops of dead pine trees on opposite sides of Bass creek near Willet pond. The farthest nest is occupied by the owls. The second nest is about one quarter of a mile away and clearly visible from the first. This may present a problem, for it is well known that Great Horned owls do not tolerate nests of other raptors anywhere near their own nest.

How this drama will play out remains to be seen, but I promise to reveal each installment right up to the final denouement.

Osprey—Owl Update.

As summer approaches, all seems harmonious between the Great horned owl and Osprey nests near Willet pond. Indeed, a second pair of Ospreys is building a new nest even nearer the owl nest. This pair obviously is inexperienced. The nest looks like a small haystack had been whirled up by a tornado and deposited in the tree. Even as I watched, the male alighted on the back of the female in the nest shambles and looked all about for the longest time as though thinking, "Ok, I got up here, now what am I supposed to do?" Lets hope he gets it right and all that furious assembly of twigs was not in vain.

In Spring, Not All Romance Occurs on the Beach.

In April and May a lot of strenuous romancing goes on out in the ocean off the beach. I refer to carrying-ons of the Loggerhead turtles that congregate from distances of hundreds and probably even thousands of miles, and have for millennia, in frenzies only recently mimicked by the Spring Break of our own off-spring. The most colorful and authoritative account that I have ever read was written by Archie Carr who spent so many years observing and protecting sea turtles in Central America and the Caribbean. He wrote as follows:

"Sea turtles in love are appallingly industrious. It is not easy to observe their conduct because observations come only in snatches, when the turtles rise on wave crests. But the male turtle obviously makes an awful nuisance of himself. Why the female puts up with such treatment is hard to understand. To hold himself in the mating position on top of the smooth, curved, wet, wave-tossed shell of the female, the male employs a three-point grappling rig, consisting of his long, thick, recurved, horn-tipped tail, and a heavy, hooked claw on each front flipper. Sea turtles breath air of course so both sexes naturally try to stay at the surface during the violent mating engagement. This adds to the acrobatic problems of the male, and augments his intemperate scraping and thrashing at the shell of his intended. Besides all that, the female generally stays coy and resistant for what seems an unnecessarily long while. During that time other males gather, and all strive together over the female in a huge, frothy melee in which nothing, as I said, can be seen from shore except that it is pretty exciting."

After the furor subsides, the males disperse into the vastness of the ocean. The females remain for the summer and each lays her first nest about 30 days after mating. She continues to store the sperm for fertilization of subsequent clutches for the three or four nests laid during the three month nesting season. Then she too departs to roam paths not to be fathomed by mankind.

Swallows Make Good Use of the Golf Course Bridges.

In spring and early summer, golfers may note some sort of swallows flitting over the water near bridges across the lagoons. These are Barn swallows that, with a brief glance, appear as small dark birds with pointed wings and long forked tails. If you pause to observe them more carefully, especially as they dart past close to the bridge, you will be able to observe the deep blue of the back and cinnamon color of the underparts. These colors are striking if you can pick up the swift birds in the binoculars—a real test of your skill.

Barn swallows probably nested in crevices in cliffs and in caves before the arrival of man, but now they have relocated their nests almost entirely in man-made buildings, especially in barns and beneath bridges. These nests, lined with feathers and soft plant materials, adhere to the vertical and horizontal structures. They are constructed with mud from the lagoon bank and some grass for reinforcement. The swallows arrive around the first of May with courtship on their minds. It is possible to observe this for the birds perch on the bridge railings and obviously form up into pairs. Frequently the pair will rise together and soar a hundred or more feet into the air with a peculiar fluid twittering to each other. Once the bond is established, nest building begins, or they may reuse the nest of the previous year with a little renovation.

Egg laying begins a few days later and one egg is laid each day until the clutch builds up to the average of five eggs. Then the female assumes most of the task of incubation, and she takes care to turn the eggs each time she returns to the nest so that they are uniformly warmed. In two weeks the eggs hatch and then both parents are busy from dawn till dusk bringing to the hungry young the insects they catch in their swooping flights low over the lagoons.

After a month in the nest, the juveniles will begin to try their wings but will stay close to the nest and fully expect to be fed on a regular basis. You may be able to distinguish the juveniles as they loaf with the adults on the bridge rails. Their tail feathers are noticeably shorter. It is at this time that considerable jousting and pecking occurs as new orders of dominance are established. Often the dominant bird will chitter with open bill at its neighbor, who will admit submission by turning its head away. Meanwhile the parents, bored with all this scuffling and tired of feeding these big youngsters, may return to the nest for a second brood.

The parents do not seem alarmed as the golf carts rumble overhead because seldom will any dart out from beneath the bridge at such times. What they tell the youngsters is anyone's guess—after all its no worse than the trains roaring by on the El in some of our cities. I can just see the chicks clinging to the nest as the carts rumble overhead and the wooden structure sways and vibrates.

By September the last of them will pack up for fall migration. It is at this time that large flocks from farther north may pause on our beach for rest and refueling. Sometimes they also may feed as they fly, for they migrate by day at low elevation. Many of them will continue the flights as far south as Argentina where they will find new hordes of insects in the summertime of the southern hemisphere.

Some of Our Foxes Survived the Distemper Epidemic

Security patrols at night have sighted several foxes on the dark roadways, and I have observed tracks of foxes in the foredunes. Therefore, some foxes survived the canine distemper epidemic and may restore the population over the next few years. This restoration may already be in progress, because foxes breed in late February and March. The young are born sometime in May and you might see young ones following momma by mid- summer. Won't it be nice to once again catch sight of them going about their business on our island?

The Whale That Will Not Stay Down.

In an earlier story, I wrote of a twelve foot pilot whale that had washed ashore at the east end of the island. At that time Wayne McFee and his team of co-workers from the National Marine Fisheries Service came over from Ft Johnson to do an autopsy that involved, among other things, the removal of the head of the animal. After they left, I supervised as a huge front-end loader was cautiously driven out at low tide to bury the carcass. With one eye on the rising tide, the driver dug the trench and buried the whale beneath 3-4 feet of sand. Then we all forgot about it.

At the end of the year I received a report from Pat Pendery and Elsie Meyer that some sort of a fish or other strange creature had washed ashore at the east end. Again I went out and lo and behold there was a whale on the beach at about the position of the one in February. And surprisingly, it had no head. Again Wayne McFee came out and as we stood beside it speculating as to how it might have lost its head, the brain cells began to function; we sheepishly turned to one another with faces flushed with embarrassment. Yes, it was the same whale. Neither of us could understand how it had come up through all that sand or how it could be so well preserved after a year's time beneath the sand. Wayne put it back down with some vigorous shoveling. But the whale was not through, and within a month it was back on the surface. After talking to a number of people and much speculation, my best account is that a whale, with its thick layer of blubber under the skin is quite resistant to decay when beneath the moist sand and not exposed to air. The best account of its rise through the sand is that it was buried on a low sandbar between the ocean and a tidal slough so that seawater flowed beneath the sand at each high tide and raised the water table. All through the spring, summer, fall and into the winter, those twice daily rises in the water table nudged the whale slowly up though the sand until it rested again on the surface.

We decided to leave the whale where it seems to want to be and let nature take its course. Within two months on the surface and exposed to beach weather, deterioration has been rapid and the carcass now is reduced to a dry husk scarcely distinguishable from nearby driftwood.

Tree Swallows in Passage

Those blizzards of swallows that swirled by the hundreds over our lagoons in late April were Tree swallows on their northern migration. Only a few will remain to nest in South Carolina.

A Sea Turtle Nest Is A Mad Scramble
at Hatching Time.

It always seems somehow miraculous that turtle hatchlings are able to make their way up through about 18 inches of packed beach sand and escape the nest for their journey to the sea. Dr. Archie Carr, the grand old man of sea turtle conservation and research, whose interests centered on the green turtle at Totuguero, Costa Rica, described the process in an amusing way in his book about sea turtles, rather cryptically entitled "So Excellent A Fishe." During his studies in Costa Rica, he and his staff relocated a nest with a glass panel fitted into one side. At hatching, he reports as follows what they observed:

"The first young that hatch do not start digging at once but lie still until some of their nestmates are free of the egg. Each new hatchling adds to the working space, because the spherical eggs and the spaces between them make a volume greater than that of the young and the crumpled shells. The vertical displacement that will carry the turtles to the surface is the upward migration of this chamber, brought about by the witless collaboration that is really a loose sort of division of labor. Although the movements involved are only a generalized thrashing, similar to those that free the hatchling from the egg, they accomplish four different and indispensable things, depending on the position of the turtle in the mass. Turtles of the top layer scratch down the ceiling. Those around the sides undercut the walls. Those on the bottom have two roles, one mechanical and the other psychological: they trample and compact the sand that filters down from above, and they serve as a sort of nervous system for the hatchling superorganism, stirring it out of recurrent spells of lassitude. Lying passively for a time under the weight of its fellows, one of them will suddenly burst into a spasm of squirming that triggers a new pandemic of work in the mass. Thus, by fits and starts, the ceiling falls, the floor rises, and the roomful of collaborating hatchlings is carried toward the surface.

"The turtle siblings thus appear to operate as a survival group; a group, the members of which, by instinctive, generalized, and wholly non-altruistic actions help one another to survive. The little survival band is not trained or prompted by any coach, nor does it consciously work toward any common end. It is just a lot of baby turtles getting restless and becoming annoyed with one another, but in useful ways. Their petulance at being crowded, jostled, and trod upon makes them flail about aimlessly. It is the aimless flailing that takes them steadily up to the surface of the ground."

Watching the Feeder Is Only Half the Fun.

The beauty and vivacity of wild birds at the feeder is a constantly rewarding experience for many of us. If we go beyond these casual observations and attempt to understand how birds interact with one another and why they behave as they do, we encounter a totally different challenge that requires patient observation. Each bird is a conscious being that is continually responding to everything around it and communicating with others of its species. Let's illustrate with a familiar bird, the Northern cardinal. I choose the cardinal because all of us readily distinguish the sexes: the male in its bright red plumage, cocky crest and black face-mask; the female, more subdued in shades of tan and brown. Also, the juvenile cardinal is easily distinguished by its black beak, in contrast to the orange beaks of the adults.

Singing is the first characteristic that most of us associate with bird behavior. An excellent indication that your feeder will attract cardinals is the sound of their singing in your yard or that of a neighbor. We often assume that only the male of a species sings to establish territory; however, both male and female cardinals sing. The varied songs convey messages that are important in the social organization of the species and the interactions between a mated pair. The basic cardinal song is a combination of clear whistled phrases. Persons with better hearing than mine state that these phrases vary, and that counter-singing occurs. One bird will sing a phrase several times, then a second bird will match the phrase in response; the leader will sing a new phrase, again, the other will match it. This is often done between a mated pair and appears to strengthen the bond. At other times, it may occur between males, and seems to help settle territorial disputes.

Other calls, such as the chip-call—a short, metallic "chip"— frequently may be heard repeatedly while the bird is at the feeder. When this is accompanied by a raised crest and a quick upward jerk of the tail, it is commonly interpreted by bird watchers as an expression of alarm for possible danger. In other circumstances, the same chip call, when accompanied by the body language of a lowered, crouched body, head thrust forward with crest lowered and bill partially open is reputed to be an aggressive signal. It warns others not to intrude on the feeder space. Certainly, the apprehensive and frequent casting of an eye toward the sky, so common to all birds, is a precaution against the approach of a predatory raptor.

If you have a pair of cardinals at your feeder and the male feeds the female they are probably nesting close by. Later in the season this romatic touch may wear thin; I have seen the male gorge on a dozen sunflower seeds with the female begging for attention, and then finally he will descend to give her a token seed before departing. Or even worse, he will leave without even that—then you know the nesting season must be about over. (Since this was written, a male and a female came to my feeder and the female fed the male! This has implications that I have not yet had the courage to explore.)

Territoriality is very important at nesting time, and at times of intrusion by other cardinals males will chase males and females will chase females while the mate acts as a passive spectator. In the case of males, the chases may be interspersed with counter-singing bouts and chip-calls in the aggressive crouched posture. With clues such as these, it is easy to distinguish the pair that defend the feeder territory from neighboring cardinals. For example, my cardinal pair each year must contend with another pair from the opposite side of the lagoon. When I see a cardinal fly across the lagoon to my feeder I know that very shortly there will be a chase with "my" cardinal driving the other back across the lagoon and then quickly returning.

When the immature birds leave the nest, they are easily identified at the feeder by their black beaks. Usually the male cardinal feeds them as they crouch nearby giving their begging wing flutter. The last clutch occurs around the end of August, and by then the male is tired of this feeding too. Consequently, he may eat and depart, leaving it to the hungry juveniles to find their way to the feeder platform. Not all can crowd onto the feeder at once though, for the pecking order that was established in the nest still remains. More than one at the feeder at a time leads to much aggressive signalling, chip-calls and low squalling calls that seem to be peculiar to the fledglings.

Other species of birds have their own set of calls and postures for communication. Watch carefully; a review of the notes that you keep will permit you to better understand the species of particular interest to you.

Combat!

Early one lovely morning in the month of May, I was biking along the path beside Governor's Drive in the vicinity of Egret pond, when I encountered two lizards locked in combat at the edge of the path. The two were Broadhead skinks, the largest lizard in the state and fairly common on Kiawah. It is the

brown lizard that is by concensus the most unattractive of all our anoles and skinks. The males have a broad head with eyes so dark and recessed that they appear to have been burned into the skull, and during the breeding season the skin over the head turns an orange-red.

The two males, each about one foot in length were locked in combat over the usual things males fight about. Facing one another, each had a firm grip on the shoulder of the other, but their jaws were not powerful enough to pierce the scaly skin of the opponent. Driving against the other, they swirled around like a flaming pinwheel with the long tails streaming out on the perimeter. At other times the gyration ceased, and as they pressed against each other their efforts were reflected in the tremors of their bodies. It became evident that each was striving to lift the other and flip it over, but they were so evenly matched that, when one flipped the other, both ended on their backs. Then they would quickly disengage, right themselves and rush together once again.

In my imagination, I was transformed back to the era when their ancestors, the multi-ton dinosaurs, were locked in similar combat. In my mind's eye, I could see the acres of trampled vegetation, the thundering vibration of the earth as one of the huge bodies slammed down and the scurrying of the tiny mammals that were my ancestors as they fled in terror of being trampled and squashed.

Returning with relief to my towering height above the fray, I could see that they were so evenly matched that the outcome would depend upon which had the greatest stamina. Finally, one did prevail, grasped the head of the other in its jaws and threw its body over its opponent. After a minute or so, either the loser relaxed or the victor slackened its grip, and the two separated. The victor remained in place; the loser ran to the middle of the road where it sank down in a sunny spot on the yellow stripe.

Only now did the victor become aware of the wheel of my bike only a foot away and my body looming above. It froze in apprehension as though trying to readjust its moment of triumph to one of terror. And I for the first time had to assess my role in the matter. Should I just pedal off, or should I play the role of God and influence the outcome? I chose the latter role on the basis that humans had built the road and the vehicle that might at that moment be approaching to crush the exhausted loser. Backing off slowly, I left the victor to savor victory; riding toward the loser, I frightened it into the grass on the opposite side of the road. I knew that anything else I might encounter on my ride would not match the ferocity of that battle.

A Chain of Volunteers for
One Distressed Chick.

In the middle of May a young hawk was rescued by a chain of concerned individuals in a manner that illustrates so well the splendid cooperation and concern for the welfare of birds and other animals on the island, both by residents and by employees. The first hero of the story was Daryl Crabtree, an employee of Ravenel Associates. He observed a young bird standing forlornly at the edge of Kiawah Beach Drive by the West Beach Tennis Club. It apparently had fallen from its nest and was in great peril beside that busy thoroughfare. The bird had a large, hooked beak and over-size talons that signaled *raptor*, and fluffy plumage that signaled *chick*. He placed it in a box from his van and took it to the Security gate. From there, Captain Doris Simpson relayed it to Jean Howe, a member of the newly formed Wildlife Committee of the town. Jean in turn passed it on to Jim Elliott of the Charleston Raptor Center, and the Red-shoulder hawk, as it was by then identified, received expert care in the form of rehydration, nourishment and rest. It recovered quickly, and the next step was to restore it to the wild.

Jim Elliott called me and suggested that we try to place it back in its nest. I located the nest close to where the chick had been found; it was deep in the interior of a Live oak tree and well concealed by a drapery of Spanish moss. Meanwhile, Dylan Jones of the Recreation Department became aware of the tragedy, and had inquired of the Johns Island Fire department whether they could provide a ladder for the relocation. Fire Marshal Lester Sadler arrived and after viewing the nest informed me that it would be no problem for them to relocate the bird. However, I by then had foreseen another problem. As I watched the nest, the parent arrived to feed the remaining two chicks that were about ¾ fully grown. As the three big birds jostled about in the rather small nest during the feeding, I could see that the fallen chick, which was the runt of the clutch, would probably be out of the nest and back on the ground within a few hours.

Jim Elliott and I discussed the problem and Jim agreed that the chick could not be returned to the nest. However, another option had become available. A slightly larger Red-shoulder hawk chick had been rescued in Summerville a few days earlier under similar circumstances. It had been restored to its nest and promptly booted out again. Jim proposed that the two orphans be united and reared in a hacking structure. Hacking is now a rather common and quite successful procedure for restoring chicks and injured birds to the wild. It is done in this way. An elevated shelter for the chicks is closed on three sides and fitted with bars on the fourth side. A nest is formed inside the box and the chicks are placed within it. Feeding is done surreptitiously so that the chicks do not form an attachment for humans.

Once the chicks develop to the point of fledging, the bars are removed. When I talked with Jim late in June, both the young hawks were doing fine. They are free to depart and are learning to forage for food, but they still return frequently to the "nest." They require less feeding each day and Jim expects them to soon be truly back in the wild state. Therefore, this fortunate chick, through a chain of actions by at least seven or eight concerned humans, will have the opportunity for life; an opportunity that would have been forever denied it, had it been left abandoned on that busy roadway.

Alligator Nesting at Bufflehead Pond.

A seven-foot-long alligator has chosen to build her nest beside the bench at the western end of Bufflehead pond. Now, much of her time is spent lying low in the water 10 or 20 feet offshore, like a partially submerged gray log, as she watches her nest. These nests are constructed by the female from pond vegetation and mud that she carries in her mouth and shapes with her body to form a mound about 5 feet across and 2 feet high. (From a safe distance, the nest by the bench is well camouflaged to look like a pile of dead reeds and grasses.)

The alligator then makes a depression in the top of the mound and deposits about 40 leathery, white eggs that resemble goose eggs. Those who have watched the egg-laying process state that as each egg leaves her body, she meets it with the underside of her hind limb, first breaking the fall and then positioning the egg in the nest. After the last egg has been deposited, she covers the clutch; with amazing control, she grasps vegetation with the claws of her hind limb and lays it over the eggs. And there they will incubate over the next two months.

We should always remember that alligators are better mothers than the turtles that nest on the beach. The alligator remains nearby throughout the incubation period just as this alligator is now doing, and she challenges all intruders, including raccoons and humans. Therefore, she should have exclusive rights to that bench for the rest of the summer.

The Nature of Our Beach

Our beach is responsive to both wind and water currents as is to be expected of anything made of sand. In general, winter storms erode the beach, and the sand is widely distributed both above and below the low tide line to form a long, flat beach. The shallow slope resists the force of incoming waves and thus is a form of protection from further damage. More gentle waves of summer restore the dunes by acting in concert with the wind to drive the sand back up into the dunes. These modest changes are to be expected annually, and some fall and winter storms even cut steep banks which later heal as the sand dries and the banks collapse in the spring under the influences of wind and wave.

However, some changes may have a more profound, long-term effect on the size and shape of the beach. The most dramatic change within historical times occurred in the period 1862 - 1921. It was during that period that jetties were constructed at the entrance to Charleston Harbor (1878-96). One serious consequence was the change of the offshore currents and extensive erosion of the beaches of Folly and Morris islands. The eroded sand moved southward due to prevailing ocean currents and much of it was deposited at the eastern end of Kiawah. Professor Miles O. Hayes and his students at the USC Geology department studied the Kiawah beach at the time of the Environmental Inventory of Kiawah Island in 1975. They determined that the eastern end of the island had advanced 3,400 ft by the early 1940's.

The shoreline at the east end of the island still fluctuates in response to the periodic accumulation of sand shoals in the ebb tidal delta of the Stono Inlet. When a shoal builds up, the ocean current that normally runs from east to west and parallel to the beach may be deflected landward and erosion may occur at the center of the beach. After these shoals migrate and attach along the easternmost mile of Kiawah's shoreline, sand is distributed all along the beach, and the damage usually is corrected.

At the present time a large shoal has accumulated at the Stono Inlet and we are seeing the resulting erosion in the midsection of the beach, particularly in the area of East Beach Village (Windswept Villas). When this shoal attaches to the eastern end of Kiawah, the central beach should be restored, for the overall impact of shoal attachments has been positive for Kiawah. Just in the past half century, the state Coastal Council estimates that over 12 million cubic yards have been gained along the Kiawah beach as a result of sand deposition from these shoals. Another way of viewing this is that the shoals are an immense reservoir of sand for natural renourishment of the beach after storms.

Ocean currents and storms often cut inlets through the central portion of long barrier islands such as Kiawah, and two have existed here for a very long time—indeed they are shown on the first known chart of the island, dated 1661. These two inlets are located in the regions that are now Ibis and Willet ponds. (You might like to refer to the map on page 122.) When the inlets existed, tidal flow occurred between the ocean and Bass creek on the Kiawah river side of the island. Therefore, Otter and Cougar were truly islands and separate from the main island we call Kiawah. Creation of a dike as a portion of a road for hauling timber in the 1950's resulted in closure of the inlet at Ibis pond; and a similar dike at what was to become Willet pond caused the second inlet to close sometime between the aerial photographs made in 1963 and in 1973.

We can be thankful for these changes, because we now have one of the best of the barrier island beaches in the state. The Annual State of the Beaches Report of the S.C. Coastal Council dated May, 1993 tersely states, "Kiawah is one of the most stable islands in the state, although the eastern and western ends of the island are more dynamic due to their proximity to inlets. Development on Kiawah is set well landward of the primary dune line." Thank you for those kind words. Lets do what we can to keep the beach that way for all to enjoy for a very long time.

Where Are All the Frogs?

Among the many worries of biologists these days is the concern over the disappearance of many species of frogs and decreases in frog populations worldwide. Much speculation is swirling about in scientific meetings on such matters. Based on my recent observations, I may need to attend and give my own theory, which is that frogs have developed a craze for motor cars and are just not able to handle it. Takes you back to Mr Toad of Toad Hall in the delightful story "The Wind in the Willows" by Kenneth Grahame that we all read or were read to as children. But let me tell you the basis for my theory and you be the judge.

As I was washing the beach sand and salt off my little blue pickup truck one afternoon, I noticed a frog peering out from beneath the small door that is supposed to close off the gasoline compartment (some things on my truck do not fit together as tightly as they did six years ago.) At my approach, it leaped down onto the drive and I noted before it hopped off into the shrubbery that it was a tan frog about 1 ¼ inches long in crouched dimension. For those of you unsatisfied with this description, my guidebook later informed me it was a Squirrel treefrog that is rather common in the lowcountry.

I thought nothing further about it until a week later when I had occasion to get gas at the Village store. As I opened the flap, out jumped what I feel sure was the identical frog. By now I felt some obligation to the creature and couldn't just leave it in such a hazardous location. I pursued it for some time about the pump bases and fuel lines and finally retrieved it at the feet of a burly construction worker at another pump. No words seemed adequate so with a friendly but rather feeble smile I returned to my pump. By now rather disgruntled, I tossed the frog unceremoniously into the back of the truck and pumped my gas. As I started into the store, the frog was on the top edge of the bed liner and I flipped it off into some juniper bushes.

When I returned "my" frog was back on the curb looking at the truck. Without much thought, I picked it up, and it offered no evasive resistance as though it now accepted me as co-owner of the vehicle. I tossed it into the passenger seat and was on my way. Mr. Frog went up the window for a better view, turned green with the thrill of it all, and then sat for a time in my lap. Finally it may have longed for the comfort and view from the gas tank for it went up the partially open window, and despite my warnings went over the edge and disappeared. I fear it is now but a small grease spot in the road, but knowing its love for motoring and its determination, I wouldn't be surprised to see it peeking out from beneath the flap again any day.

Continued Saga of Least Tern Nesting: The Westend Story

You may recall that in a story for Summer, 1994, I told you that the Least tern nests in colonies on exposed beaches along our east coast. Increasingly, this habitat has become unavailable as humans usurp the beaches, and the terns are resorting to nesting on flat rooftops. I have been interested since the early 1980's in the welfare of the two colonies that historically had nested on Kiawah, and in that earlier story I told of the misfortunes of colonies at the eastern end in recent times (sites A and B in Figure 1). I promised then to tell you how the colony that had nested historically at the western end of Kiawah (at site C in that figure) was lured away to nest on Seabrook Island. So, here is my sequel, the "Westend Story."

In 1983 the western colony at site C in the left portion of Figure 2 was disrupted by the rechannelization of the Kiawah river as shown in the right-hand portion of that figure. Dredging had started in mid-February and by the time the terns arrived in early May the profile of the sand deposition at the eastern end of Seabrook and western end of Kiawah had changed from that on the left to that on the right portion of the figure. What would the terns do? With no apparent hesitation, they followed the sand and nested that year at site C which was now on Seabrook Island.

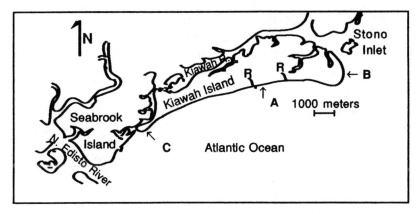

Figure 1. Diagrammatic map of the Kiawah-Seabrook area.

I followed the progress of the nesting success on Seabrook over the next few years. The character of the site changed

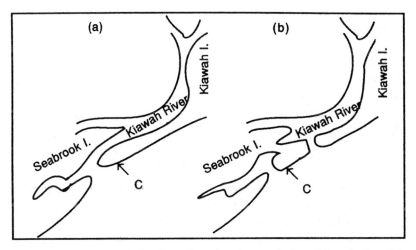

Figure 2. Diagram of the Kiawah-Seabrook area before (a) and after (b) rechannelization of the Kiawah River.

significantly with changes in ocean and river-outlet currents, redeposition of sand, and accumulation of vegetation By 1986, the colony was still trying to cope with a continually degrading terrain. It started out that year quite large and I followed its progress. This was not as easy an assignment as might at first appear, for despite their dainty appearance, these terns are very aggressive. They drive off any passing gull, heckle Ghost crabs that wander in the area, and dive-bomb invading humans with amazing accuracy. As I counted nests, eggs and chicks, I wore what I termed my "Tern Suit" complete with wide-brimmed hat. Suffice to say, the Tern Suit was never allowed in our house except to go directly to the laundry.

The colony built up to 135 nests, although it was disturbed frequently by people crossing it on their walks along the beach, by their free-running dogs, and by saddle horses and security vehicles. No malicious damage was noted but the terns harassed them all as potential predators. Then, as hatching was underway the entire site was tidally overwashed in a storm and only 13 nests survived.

I continued to monitor the colony during following seasons. For 1987, 69 nests were observed on Seabrook but the colony was again completely destroyed by a severe storm on June 4th. One nest was found in 1988 and none in 1989-91 although numerous terns were seen flying over the area. Then, in 1992, the colony was reestablished at the western end of Kiawah. In part this may have been due to the unfavorable habitat of the Seabrook beach, and in part because the western end of Kiawah was once again extending toward Seabrook as sand deposited and was washed westward by the prevailing ocean current. Forty two nests were estimated to be present in mid-season, but here too disaster struck; a heavy rain combined with strong tides flooded the entire colony on June 12th.

Since then, there have been only sporadic attempts to nest on either Seabrook or Kiawah. Although the terns nested on the more favorable beach in the center of Kiawah even in the early 1980's, the increased disturbance by human activities forced them to the less populated ends of the island. The unfavorable low terrain there has repeatedly lead to destruction through flooding. What to do? Evidently the terns have been driven to the only alternative they have found; the rooftops in the Charleston area. The question for the future will be what this species can do when mankind ceases to build flat roofs with tar & gravel surfaces?

The Kemp's Ridley Sea Turtle.

At the end of May, I had the sad task of identifying a small marine turtle that washed ashore dead. From the pattern of shell plates, called scutes, I identified it as a Kemp's ridley (*Lepidochelys kempi*), the smallest of all the existing species of sea turtles. Its heart- shaped carapace was just 18" long and 20" broad. This particular species of the ridley cruises the shallow continental shelf of the Gulf of Mexico and up along the Atlantic shore as it feeds on crabs and molluscs. Its closely related cousin, the Olive ridley occurs on the Pacific side—just across the Isthmus of Panama—and it is interesting to speculate that in earlier times a single ridley species evolved into two separate species after the Isthmus was created as a barrier between the two oceans.

The Kemp's ridley differs from other sea turtles in that it comes ashore during the daytime to nest in immense groups called arribadas. This was first observed in 1947 at a beach near Rancho Nuevo about 100 miles below the Texas border with Mexico. This may now be the only nesting site in the world for the species, and the number of nesting females have dwindled to a few hundred. There is some hope that because of this unusual concentration of nesting at a single beach, the site can be protected well enough that the population may be restored. But at present, the Kemp's ridley is just hanging onto the edge of the precipice above extinction.

The one that washed ashore was moderately decomposed and probably had drifted about for days and possibly weeks. It was missing one flipper that may have been lost to a shark after death. In the absence of an obvious injury, no cause of death could be assigned, but drowning in a fisherman's net is likely. Protection of that single nesting beach may not be adequate for the species when these other dangerous encounters with humans enters into the balance.

Rhythms of the Tidalmarsh.

It is worth emphasizing *tidal* in tidalmarsh for the existence of the marsh and the behavior of all plant and animal life that dwells there must adjust to the daily rhythm of the tides. For example, the fiddler crabs actively search for food and mates at low tide, but as the water rises, they dash down, each to its own burrow, plug the entrance with mud and wait out the high tide.

Other animals that live on the marsh or come to it for food and shelter must also conform to the tidal rhythm. As the tide rises, animals such as the raccoons, field mice and cotton rats retreat to high ground. The periwinkle snails that have been grazing on the algae climb stalks of spartina to avoid the water and the predators that come in with the rising water. Those that enter with the tide include the mud crabs and blue crabs to scavenge the organisms that did not escape the rising water. Also, the tidal inflow brings into the marsh the many larval stages of fish, shrimp and crab. Abundant food and refuge from predators make the marsh an ideal nursery ground. The large, predatory fish dare not penetrate the dense stand of spartina, for those that do often become entrapped and perish when the water recedes. Their bodies in turn are consumed at the change of the tide by the returning land animals.

The tidal creeks offer a different habitat. Here, the large predatory fish such as red drum, spotted seatrout and flounder enter with the inflow of tidal water, but they also must be careful to retreat in time to avoid the muddy waters of the low-tide rivulets where temperatures soar and dissolved oxygen levels plunge. Two interesting mammals time their visits for the high tide. One is the dolphin that comes up the creeks from the Kiawah river. These seemingly happy-go-lucky characters pursue the fish and herd them up on the mud banks for easy capture. Others take advantage of the sudden bonanza, and even the timid Sora rail may dash from the cover of the grass beds to snatch up a tidbit. Occasionally, a dolphin will misjudge the tide and become stranded. But usually, they somehow manage to survive until the next tide lifts them free.

The other mammal is truly a marsh animal, it is the otter. It too enters the creeks at high tide for it does not seem to enjoy trudging about over the oyster shells and bottom muck. When the tide comes in, however, it leaves the lagoon, bounds along over the dike and into the creek. You will know if it is around, because it is a creature of habit and forms a well-worn path on each side of the dike bank.

Most of the birds that visit the marsh adjust their arrival to match their method of feeding and the prey they seek. Laughing gulls in search of fiddler crabs wait for the low tide to soar over the roaming bands of crabs. Also, the egrets and herons await the low tide to patrol the creek beds, for then the fish and crabs are concentrated in shallow pools and are easy prey. By contrast, the migratory ducks in winter prefer the creeks at high tide, and they depart for the river, ocean or inland ponds as the water recedes. However, some of the birds that are permanent residents of the marsh seem to be active at any tide. These would include the Clapper rail that you are more likely to hear than to see as it glides stealthily between the grass stalks. It really deserves its name for it is "thin as a rail."

Other rhythms, also determined by solar events, proceed more slowly. I refer to the seasonal changes as planet earth wobbles in its orbit around the sun. With the shorter days of fall, creek fauna decline both in total numbers and species diversity. Organisms that developed and grew during spring and summer now have matured sufficiently to leave the shelter of the marsh. Even some of the permanent residents retreat temporarily to deeper and warmer waters in the estuary during severe winter weather. Like the endless cycle of the tides, creatures of the marsh ebb and flow with the seasons. So too, does the marsh grass, for the spartina stalks darken and die to add to the mulch that will be needed in the coming spring. But even as they die back, sprouts of new growth rise from the perennial roots to create the marsh of the coming year.

Another Tough Year for the Ospreys.

In an earlier story last spring I expressed concern as to whether owls and ospreys could be good neighbors. From subsequent observations, the answer is emphatically <u>No</u>. You may recall that a pair of Great Horned owls nested in the old osprey nest high in a dead pine snag on the little island across Bass creek. That island is heavily wooded with tall pines and a dense underbrush of myrtles and low saw-tooth palmettos; an ideal nesting habitat for any animal wishing to be left alone. When the two fluffy brown chicks were half-grown in April, they both disappeared from the nest overnight, and I assumed that they had fluttered down on stubby wings to the undergrowth. It had happened the year before, and I had located the chicks as related in the spring of 1993. This rather odd behavior is common with this species; it may be an acquired trait that removes the chicks from the exposed nest as soon as possible. The owl family probably remained on the little island all this spring; it is known that the parents continue to feed the chicks into early summer and well past the time they are capable of flight. To the busy owl parents, plump osprey chicks in exposed nests high in nearby pine snags must present tempting targets.

This brings us to the osprey nestings, of course. As I mentioned earlier, two osprey nests were made within a quarter of a mile of the owl nest. The first nest to become active and the one farthest from the owls, contained three fluffy, gray chicks early in May. Their bobbing little heads could be seen over the rim of the nest as the parent fed them. On May 27th only one half-grown chick was seen close by the parent who was perched on the rim. When I checked two days later, the nest was empty and one osprey parent was perched in a spindly pine tree several hundred feet away. Apparently, the owls had taken them all.

By the end of the month, the deserted nest began to look strangely shabby. It seems that ospreys don't just build a nest at the beginning of the season and then use it rent-free. No, maintenance and restoration must go on all through the season.

I first realized this while I was observing the same nest earlier, on a happier day, when chicks were present; one of the parents several times brought small branches to the nest. Pushing the inquisitive chicks aside, she proceeded to work the branches into the nest with much rearranging.

What of the other osprey nest, the one built by the inexperienced pair as described in the spring story? By the time the female settled down over eggs, the nest had assumed a presentable appearance. It was located lower than the first, in the middle of a living pine tree. Would it be better protected from those ravenous owls?

Early in June two healthy chicks were to be seen weaving about on weak legs. On the first of July, the family looked fine; the chicks were about half grown and well feathered in the plumage of the juvenile stage. On their backs the speckled tan and dark brown plumage matched amazingly well the pattern and colors of a pine cone beside them in the nest. I wonder whether this is coincidental or another example of nature's camouflage for a species that so frequently nests in pine trees? One parent, stationed on a branch above the nest, and both chicks continually scanned the sky and tracked each passing bird. Sometimes I could tell that they were watching a bird beyond my range of vision. When a Red-tail hawk passed in the vicinity of the nest the parent dropped to the nest rim while calling loudly, and the two chicks crouched in the bottom of the nest. It became apparent to me that this family was vigilant for any threat, and I was increasingly optimistic for their success.

When both chicks fledged later in July, I knew that we had a successful nesting despite the owls. It would be only speculative to seek the reason for the success. It might have been the safer nest location, more vigilance by the ospreys or simply that the owl family had broken up and was hunting elsewhere. Whatever the cause, it was gratifying for me to follow a complete nesting after a decade of unsuccessful attempts by so many osprey pairs.

In Winter, Many of Our Birds Travel in Mixed Flocks

In winter, we often observe the daily movement of small flocks, composed of several bird species, traveling together and moving between the yards and through the woods as they search the bare branches for any remaining insects and berries. These mixed flocks may appear to be simply casual gatherings of the resident birds; but banding of the birds and careful observation has demonstrated that the flocks are tightly organized.

The nucleus of the flock is composed of the titmice and chickadees. The same individuals band together each morning and are soon joined by a host of followers that may include several warblers and usually a single woodpecker—often the Hairy woodpecker. The tiny chickadees essentially lead the flock as they forage for food and maintain a definite winter territory. This territory is usually centered about the summer territory of one nesting pair of chickadees, but it is about twice as large as the summer territory. When another flock trespasses, aggressive interactions follow with chases and much calling. These interactions are common and are very obvious, for the feeding flock is normally quiet as it moves along. When you hear aggressive calls, it is a signal that there is a boundary conflict; when the flock becomes quiet again, it means the conflict has been resolved. The follower species are often less tightly associated with the territory and may freely pass from one group of chickadees to another. A relatively scarce species such as the Hairy woodpecker may join in the activities of several of these flocks while maintaining its own winter territory against other Hairy woodpeckers.

The question arises as to what advantages these mixed flocks offer the participants? Careful observation of the behavior of flocks has revealed that chickadees and titmice consistently are the first to give an alarm upon the sighting of a predatory hawk. The followers react immediately to seek concealment and therefore are the beneficiaries. Even in the absence of the predator, the follower species benefit by placing their trust in the vigilant chickadees. It has been observed that the woodpecker, for example, feeds more intensively and spends less of its time looking about for danger when in the flock then when it is foraging alone.

Another question then arises: are the chickadees and titmice altruistically protecting the followers without reciprocal benefits? The answer is that they and all other members of the flock benefit from the sheer numbers present. Their chances of survival are greater the larger the number of birds present so that they are shielded from attack by the presence of the followers that surround them.

You might think that there would be disadvantages, perhaps from all species competing for the same meager supply of food. But conflict between the species is surprisingly low, because each species has a preferred foraging niche. For example, chickadees prefer to search the lower, outer branches while the woodpecker is inspecting the trunk and main branches. So the next time a flock is passing by, look for the variety of species participating, and if you are fortunate enough to be present at the time of a territorial dispute between the chickadees, enjoy the action.

Sea Rocket
The Beach Plant That Blooms in the Winter.

Plants that grow in the dunes and especially those that can exist on the open beach must resort to special measures to survive under those harsh conditions. One of the most unusual survival tactics has been acquired by the plant called Sea-rocket (*Cakile edentule*). It has chosen to avoid the hot, dry summers by reversing its seasons and going dormant during the summer. It is such a tough contender that it is recognized globally as a pioneer genus in harsh environments. Its greatest claim to fame, for it appears in all texts on beach plants, is that it was the first vascular vegetation to appear on Iceland's newly formed volcanic island of Surtsey.

On Kiawah, a decade ago just a few plants of the species were to be found at the eastern end; now, it is common all along the beach just above the high tide line. The illustration below may help you to identify it. In spring and early summer it is the only plant close to the tide-line that has green and succulent leaves that are crenate (scalloped edges as illustrated.) By early summer the plant is well into its autumn, the leaves are yellowing and falling. Seeds sprout then at the base of the dry, gray stalks that remain. These seeds, shown to the right in the figure, also are remarkable in their adaptation for propagation of the plant for the next season. The seed is separated by a cleavage plain into basal and terminal segments, each containing a single seed. These segments permit a dual means of propagation. When mature, the seed coat is dry and corky and capable of floating great distances in the ocean. With time, the terminal segment breaks off and is the voyager. It may be carried by the ocean currents as far as Seabrook Island or even the Island of Surtsey as mentioned above. The basal segment is the homebody. It remains attached to the stalk of the old growth and with time creates a new plant at the same site.

By early winter the new green plants are pushing up in the midst of the gray stalks of the previous year. It is always a joy to find them flowering in February and March on a cold, windy beach. The wee petals of the flowers shown on the left of the figure vary from white to light pinkish purple. Watch for them but you may need to bring your magnifying glass to see details of the tiny structures.

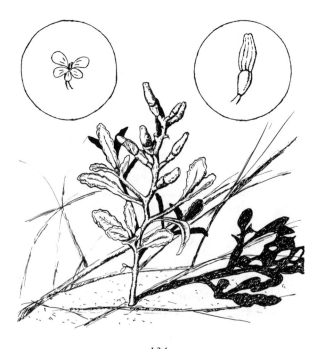

Index

A

Alligator 17, 19 - 20, 34, 52 - 53, 58, 87, 116 - 117

B

Bald eagle 17, 20, 28, 55, 59, 65, 76, 94

Beach stability25, 91

Birds:

  Behavior 51, 56, 69, 110

  Breeders 45, 55

  Migration 15, 32

  Mixed flocks 131

  Nestboxes 69

  Nesting colonies 43, 71, 103, 123

  Unusual sightins, 51, 74, 94

C

Coromorant 56 - 58

Cougar 47

D

Deer 31, 45, 49

Dolphin 35 - 37, 81 - 82, 127 - 128

Ducks:

  Ocean 27, 98

  Ponds 15, 46, 86, 94, 96

Dune Plants 41, 86, 133

F

Frogs 121

G

Gray fox 40, 66, 72, 75, 87, 92 - 93, 95, 100, 105

Great Horned Owl 28 - 29, 59, 65, 77, 101, 102, 129

Gulls 14, 43 - 44, 71, 124, 128

H

Hawk, rescue 115

History 21, 31, 35, 53, 71, 83, 90, 119

L

Least tern 71 - 72, 122

Lizards 112

M
Marsh 63, 99, 127
O
Osprey 28 - 29, 31, 59, 65, 76 - 77, 94, 101 - 102, 129 - 131
Otter 17, 34, 128
P
Pelican 43 - 44, 55 - 58, 84 - 85
Ponds 51, 56
Portuguese Man-of-War 19, 67, 69
R
Raccoon 13, 21 - 23, 38, 40, 49, 64, 66, 71 - 72, 77, 87, 92 - 93, 100, 117, 127
Rattlesnakes 9
Red knots 32
S
Snakes 9 - 11, 26
T
Turtle, Green 11
Turtle, Hawksbill 11
Turtle, Kemp's Ridley 11, 125
Turtle, Leatherback 11, 78
Turtle, Loggerhead 11 - 12, 21 - 22, 24, 37, 41, 65, 74, 94, 102, 109
W
Whales36, 60, 81, 105
White ibis 26
Wildlife: Food Sources 19
Wood storks 89